Life After Welfare

 W9-DHU-408

LIFE AFTER WELFARE

Reform and the Persistence of Poverty

Laura Lein and Deanna T. Schexnayder

With Karen Nanges Douglas and Daniel G. Schroeder

UNIVERSITY OF TEXAS PRESS   AUSTIN

Requests for permission to reproduce
material from this work should be sent to:
    Permissions
    University of Texas Press
    P.O. Box 7819
    Austin, TX 78713-7819
    www.utexas.edu/utpress/about/
    bpermission.html

♾ The paper used in this book meets the
minimum requirements of ANSI/NISO
Z39.48–1992 (R1997) (Permanence of
Paper).

Library of Congress Cataloging-in-
Publication Data
Lein, Laura.
Life after welfare : reform and the
persistence of poverty / Laura Lein and
Deanna T. Schexnayder ; with Karen
Nanges Douglas and Daniel G. Schroeder.
— 1st ed.
p. cm.
Includes bibliographical references and
index.
ISBN 978-0-292-71666-7 (cloth : alk. paper)
— ISBN 978-0-292-71667-4 (pbk. : alk.
paper)
1. Public welfare—Texas. 2. Poor families
—Texas. I. Schexnayder, Deanna. II. Title.
HV98.T5L44 2007
362.5'56809764—dc22
2007000697

To our children and

the children of the families from whom we learned so much

CONTENTS

IN 1996, THEN president Bill Clinton signed a law intended to "end welfare as we know it." President George W. Bush subsequently worked toward a reauthorization of that same bill with increasingly stringent requirements for welfare recipients; the revised bill became law in January 2006. This book examines the ways in which this new approach to welfare has played out in the lives of impoverished families in Texas who draw on welfare support. In particular, it answers the question, How are these families doing when they leave welfare?

Since the mid-1990s, many states have experimented with various types of welfare reform, and it is a well-known and highly publicized fact that the welfare rolls have declined as a result. Along with declines in the welfare rolls, the years after welfare reform saw a decline in the use of Medicaid, the public health insurance program for low-income families and their children, accompanied by an initial increase in the number of those without health insurance. Roughly half of those who left welfare were employed; of the others, some married, some became eligible for Supplemental Security Insurance or other disability support, and some we know very little about. If the goal of welfare reform was to reduce the welfare rolls, it was undeniably successful, at least in the short run. However, if the goal of welfare reform was to reduce poverty and increase the well-being

and stability of families previously on welfare, the results are far more complicated and disturbing. In this book we explore the experiences of groups of Texas
families who left welfare in the early days after the implementation of welfare
reform.

The results of welfare reform in Texas are of interest to many in Texas, but
they should also be of compelling interest to other states. At this time, policy-
makers are arguing the benefits of increasing severity in the terms of welfare
reform. The recently passed federal reauthorization bill includes stricter work
requirements and effectively no new funds for child care. Texas, with its early experiments with welfare reform and a relatively limited welfare program to begin
with, is an important arena in which to study the aftermath of welfare reform.
In many ways, Texas experimented relatively early with restrictions and more
limited benefits for welfare recipients. Through the experiences of Texas welfare
leavers, we can examine the potential outcomes of similar policy initiatives in
other states as budgetary constraints begin to affect welfare policies.

In the years following the welfare reform initiatives, many states have conducted studies to determine how the new policies affect the families they serve.
In particular, states need to learn if former welfare recipients are employed or
receiving other types of economic supports, how many have returned to welfare,
and reasons for families' success or failure. The U.S. Department of Health and
Human Services (DHHS) has supported these efforts through a number of grants
to states to conduct research on Temporary Assistance to Needy Families (TANF)
leavers. A synthesis of the findings from the first of these studies indicates that:

- Three out of five families leaving welfare are employed at any given point
  after exiting welfare. Although three-quarters of leavers have worked within
  a year of leaving welfare, their incomes cluster around the poverty level.
- A significant minority of TANF leavers return to welfare.
- More than one-third of leavers receive food stamps, and approximately 40
  percent have Medicaid coverage in the fourth quarter following exit.
- Child care findings are inconclusive, with little data available on this topic.
- Leavers still experience hardship, such as not having enough food, but evidence is mixed as to whether these events are more common before or after
  exit from TANF. (See Acs and Loprest [2001] for a full report on the findings
  from the first round of leavers grants.)

Over several years, the Texas Department of Human Services also sponsored
research to determine the status of families who left TANF after the implementation of welfare reform. This book combines the findings of this state-funded

research with those of federally funded research (through a grant from DHHS) to develop a comprehensive picture of Texas families who have left TANF. Although no one approach can fully assess the effects of welfare reform on poor families, the use of multiple approaches can provide a more complete picture of how low-income families in Texas are faring in the wake of various welfare reform initiatives.

Welfare reform is a rapidly changing arena. Since the data described in this book were collected, a number of changes have occurred in Texas welfare policy. These changes range from the introduction, success, and subsequent reduction of the Child Health Insurance Program to the development of call-in centers for the determination of program eligibility (which is being implemented in 2006). Although some of these changes promise to be of some benefit to impoverished families, there is little evidence that they will substantially change their poverty status.

ACKNOWLEDGMENTS

THE WORK DESCRIBED in this book benefited from the valuable contributions of many people. We especially recognize the work of Freddie Richards, from Prairie View A&M University, and David Dominguez, who co-authored with us the technical report on which this book is partly based.

We want to express our appreciation to the U.S. DHHS Office of Assistant Secretary for Planning and Evaluation (ASPE) and the Texas Department of Human Services (DHS) for jointly funding this research. In particular, we thank Julie Isaacs and Matt Lyon of ASPE and Elizabeth Jones and Ellen Montgomery of DHS for serving as the project officers for this research. Debora L. Morris of DHS played a major role by suggesting that we combine several research projects into one, and by managing communication about the project with its many stakeholders. Sandra Simon and Kent Gummerman also contributed to the initial stages of this project.

We thank members of this project's External Advisory Committee for participating in the planning of this project, reviewing and commenting on the preliminary report, and identifying key issues to be addressed in our research. The committee consisted of representatives of the Governor's Office, Texas Senate, Texas House of Representatives, Texas Legislative Council, Texas Workforce

Commission, Office of the Attorney General, Texas Council on Workforce and Economic Competitiveness, Texas Works Advisory Council, and the Center for Public Policy Priorities.

This book would not have been possible without the contributions of the many Texas agency staff members who helped us more clearly understand agency policies, provided the administrative data needed for our analysis, and reviewed drafts of the original technical report. Special thanks go to Irma Davila, Lea Isgur, Margaret Lane-Mendoza, Li-Chin Wu, and Dorothy Hafner, all of whom were with the DHS. At the Texas Workforce Commission, Arnold Williams, Mike Walker, Joan Kotal, Keith Athey, Jim Nolan, and Del De Los Santos provided support throughout the project period. Will Rogers, Victor Mantilla, and Iliana Ruiz from the Texas Office of the Attorney General and Pete Garza and D. Leasel Smith from the Department of Protective and Regulatory Services also provided valuable information for this project.

We particularly thank the hundreds of Texas families who agreed to meet and talk with us in person, over the telephone, and through mail surveys. Without their participation, the valuable perspective of families who applied for or participated in the TANF program would have been lost. We have changed their names throughout to protect confidentiality.

The present book was compiled from several separate research projects, and we are indebted to the large team of researchers who participated with the authors in the different constituent studies. Research staff (in addition to the authors of this book, and Freddie Richards and David Dominguez, who co-authored the original technical report) for the qualitative data and survey data collection and analysis are listed below. Many staff and faculty from several participating universities, including the University of Texas at Austin, Prairie View A&M University, the University of Texas at El Paso, and St. Edwards University, worked on more than one of the projects. They are listed here only on the first project in which they participated.

- One-Time Recipients Research: Veronica de la Garza, Greg Ellis, Yolanda Rodriguez-Escobar, Norma Salazar, and Audrey Steiner
- Texas Families in Transition Study: Adrienne Baker, Julie Beausoleil, Jenifer Bratter, Andrea Braun, Gawon Chung, Kelly Cruz, Rudy Dominguez, Elizabeth Farrington, Nancy Francisco-Stewart, Gerardo Gomez, Miguel Gomez, Edmund Gordon, Gloria Herrera, Sandy Hewamene, Stacey Jones, Alexa Lim, Rey Martinez, Jamie Mathes, Anita McClendon, Orville McNeil, David Miller, Anthony Morris, Kathleen Murphy, Anne Ogolla, Bunmi Osazuwa, Ann Pollock, Liliane Soares, Kristine Tran, Michael Trevino, and Agustin Valdivia

- Study of Denied Applicants: Tara Alexander, Cecilia Alonzo, Sally Daguer, Denise Ferrales, Robyn Lugar, Alejandro Montoya, Gustavo Perez, Mary Lou Rodriguez, and Ann Schwartz

Several colleagues from the Ray Marshall Center also contributed to this study. Chris King, the center's director, reviewed the research plan and report drafts, and Jerry Olson, chief economist, provided statistical expertise. Martha Dollar, the center's research librarian, and Leah Kegler, graduate research assistant, researched and analyzed published literature and written policies. Diane Janes managed many of the financial and procedural aspects of this project, while Karen Franke assisted in the production of the original report.

Colleagues from the Center for Social Work Research included Harriet Sullivan, Greg Whitworth, and Jennifer Earl-Graham, who tirelessly made arrangements for the project and managed financial and administrative aspects of the project. Jenifer Bratter and Julie Beausoleil contributed to the data analysis and to the editing of the report that became a major source for this book.

Without these many contributions, this book would have been impossible. That said, the final product and the interpretations presented here are the sole responsibility of the authors.

Life After Welfare

ONE

Families in a Changing Welfare Context

Sarah: Life After Welfare

WE MET SARAH, an African-American mother of four—a larger family than most on welfare—one summer Friday at a local restaurant in Houston near where she was living (all names of individuals have been changed). She brought a friend to share the lunch offered by the interviewer. Two years earlier, her husband had left her after ten years and four children together. He lived in another city, and although he had a steady job, his child support payments were infrequent. After the separation, she applied for and received aid from a governmental program, Temporary Assistance for Needy Families (TANF), for more than a year until she found a job. When we met her, she was a certified nurse's assistant, working as a home health aide for persons with mental retardation and trying to get as many hours on her job as she could in order to keep her family together. At the time we met her, she had lost the house where she had lived with her husband and was struggling to find new housing.

> I'm not on any kind of assistance. So, right now, I have to volunteer for as many hours as I can get at my job, in order to work, so, when I get through with this interview, I'll leave at 3 p.m., I'll go to work until 11:00 at night, and then I'll go to work again, from midnight to 8:00 in the morning [Saturday].

I get off Saturday morning and go back to work at 8 p.m. and get off at
8 a.m. in the morning.... I have to work at least 80 hours or plus, just to get
a $500 [two-week] paycheck. I got $600 this payday; I had 114 hours.

Although not receiving TANF, she continued to struggle with the demands of
her job, her family responsibilities, and the difficulties she faced in managing her
transitional welfare benefits. Sarah's life remained chaotic.

"You Don't Want to Wear Your Welcome Out"

Despite her long work hours, after losing her house Sarah had not been able to
save enough money to provide the down payment to lease an apartment large
enough for herself and her four children. As a result, she and her children often
stayed with friends and relatives. Although she was never without a place to
sleep, she and her children moved among households frequently.

Three weeks is a long time [to stay with someone else]. You don't want to
wear your welcome out, especially with family. Don't want to wear your welcome out. They all say they'll help, which they do. But you don't wear it out.

In addition to the stability and independence her own apartment would provide,
she needed a permanent address in order to register her children for school and
to apply for the transitional benefits of Medicaid and subsidized child care, as
well as food stamps.

I don't have a place to, to call home, to have any mail sent, or any address,
or anything like that.... I can't give welfare an address ... or apply for even
just [food] stamps. Because I just can't say where I'm going be living at, you
know, and I don't want to put somebody else in inconvenience by you tell
them "I'm living here," and then I'm really staying there for just two weeks.

She also worried that her ex-husband was evading his child support payments
as a strategy to keep her from having her own apartment, so that he might have
a better chance of gaining custody of the children.

Friends who were not able to take in her entire family were often willing to
supervise one or more of her children while she worked. However, because her
children might be shared out among several households and her work schedule
was heavy, there was less time with her children than she would have liked.

So, my typical day is no time with the kids. I don't have that much time with
them, because, the thing I always say to them, you know, "Momma's got to
go to work."

Within these constraints, Sarah still tried to arrange for real family time with her children. On occasion, Sarah made an hour-and-a-half round-trip to a family friend's home where her children could swim at a nearby pool.

Where the Money Goes

The $1,000-plus that Sarah earned from work and overtime seldom lasted the month. Although she did not pay rent, she contributed to each of the households where she stayed. As Sarah pointed out, she provided small household luxuries as well as contributions for basic necessities. If she bought her own children a treat, she provided that treat for all the children in the household, reiterating her concern not to wear out her welcome.

> You don't want to wear your welcome out at one, and then, you don't want the kids to feel so confined that they can't, they, you know, they can't go in the icebox and get what they want, or if I buy the six-pack of juices for them, or the ice cream, blow pops, or whatever, everybody else gets to eat it ... then when you move in with somebody else, you got them plus their four kids, plus whatever, so when they go in there, that's it, it's gone.

Sarah explained that having her own car was what made it possible for her to work and live in the different areas of the city as she moved from one household to another.

> I love my Suburban. Now that truck has been, for a long time, taking care of me. So then, after that, it's the best thing that I do have my "little Suburby." And it takes me out there. The only bad thing is gas. It's five dollars in and five dollars out [to her job]. And you don't play with this. That's a big truck to try to push down the hill, jump-start. And I end up borrowing the money, or like my aunt, she lent me some money.

The truck was expensive in other ways, too. Soon after making a large car insurance payment, Sarah took out a loan to cover a major repair. Several months later, she was still paying off the loan, and that payment was a continuing burden on her budget.

Dealing with regular financial demands was difficult enough, but most months she incurred unexpected additional expenses as well. During our visit, Sarah worried about how to equip her children for school. Not only did her children need basic school supplies, such as the recently mandated school uniform, she also felt it was important for their safety and personal development that they be involved in after-school activities. She had not been prepared for the related expenses.

> So, I assumed I'd get my daughter's uniform for school that she needed, at the school. You tell them to get involved in the school activities. They get involved in the school activities; school activities require that they have a certain uniform or a sweater or a jacket, and you can't get it for them. You know, so that means that they just feel bad, left out, so they don't really even want to participate. So it's hard to tell them to get involved in the school. To keep them off the streets, you try to get them involved in the school activities, and then you can't afford the uniforms for the school activities.

She was also, as we discuss later, paying for medical care and supplies. Sarah simultaneously struggled to meet the emergency and other incidental school expenses while managing her own job responsibilities and balancing her dependence on her family and friends.

The Challenges of Time-Limited Welfare

Sarah was aware that her TANF payments were time-limited (although she had not yet reached that limit), and she knew that the checks stopped once she started earning beyond the maximum allowed wage (as indeed they had some time previously). However, she was surprised by how suddenly her benefits stopped after she started working. At the same time that she lost her TANF benefits she also lost other important benefits, in part because of a missed meeting when she left the welfare office so that she could get to work on time.

> They were going to set me up for an appointment, but the caseworker cancelled because she had to go do something. Two weeks later was the only available time that they had, and this is in January, I had to go to work. And my job was like, "No, you can't do it." So I had to wait until February [to interview for TANF]. . . . I did everything they told me to do. I went to all my classes; I turned in every paperwork they asked. . . . I was doing everything they said.

Sarah never successfully reapplied for TANF, but she remained most concerned about the loss of other important benefits.

When Sarah lost her TANF coverage, she also lost her food stamps. Caught up in program regulations she found confusing and impenetrable, she was unable to reinstate these benefits. She was ineligible for emergency food stamps because she was working, and unable to access her regular food stamps once she'd been cancelled for missing an appointment. At the point that she was leaving TANF, she had not yet lost her home (although when we met her she had been without a permanent home for several months) and was still paying rent on the house she had occupied with her husband.

> Then, in December, they changed caseworkers, and I didn't get my letter [about food stamps], so, when January the first came around, I didn't get my stamps. On the second, I still didn't get my stamps. I understood that I was off TANF; I understood that part. . . . So when January came, I didn't get stamps, and that's when I went in and asked her, asked them what happened. And they told me I was cancelled. And I said, "Well, I never got a letter. Can I just reapply?" If I reapply, I have to start all over from beginning. And I asked her, "Why would I have to start over from beginning? My paperwork is in the computer from December and you just changed the caseworker. Just pull my Social Security up."
> So, in the meantime, I said, "Well, can I have emergency food stamps?" As long as I'm working, I'm not classified as an emergency. "You don't have emergency stamps because you're working." I said, "Well, I don't have any food." "What are you doing with your money?" "I'm paying the rent. You know—your $500 go for the rent, because the rent is high. You got water, you got your electricity, and you got your other basic needs, the gas. One whole check goes to rent. The other whole check goes to your basic needs, so if you buy food, it's like maybe $100. One hundred dollars worth of food is not that much for four kids and an adult.

At the same time that she left TANF and lost her food stamps, Sarah and her children also lost their medical insurance. They were dropped from Medicaid, and the Children's Health Insurance Plan (CHIP) was not yet available in Texas. Not only was Sarah confused and concerned about her family's Medicaid eligibility, she also worried about whether she could afford the medical costs associated with her children's health care needs.

> Now mind you, when, when the welfare stopped, not just the stamps, my Medicaid for the kids, everything. . . . I don't care about my Medicaid, but the kids have their little physicals they should have to take and to keep up with their shot records.

That fall, still on TANF, Sarah had planned for her daughter to have recommended dental work, including a root canal. However, the work was delayed, and by the time they arrived at the dentist's office in December, the procedure was denied because their Medicaid was no longer active. Meanwhile, Sarah struggled to obtain treatment for one child's sinus infection and another's asthma.

> December's a cold time so that's when her sinuses are really acting up, and my other daughter needed her pump for her sports starting in January and February. We couldn't get any of that. So that's when . . . I thought since TANF ended, then that's why Medicaid ended. And I couldn't get medical benefits from my job yet, because I had to be there six months.

Sarah tried to get the medical care her children needed, and the physicals and well-child checks they should have had. However, without health insurance, the costs were prohibitive.

At the time of our interview, Sarah was suffering from an untreated bladder infection. Like other indigent patients without Medicaid, her only source of treatment was the city emergency room. However, unless you are seriously sick, she pointed out, you wait for hours, and she couldn't afford to miss the hours from work, or the time away from her children should she try to go after work. Furthermore, even medical care at the city hospital required a co-payment that she was not sure she could afford.

Sarah also sought assistance through the Women, Infants and Children (WIC) food program for her three-year-old. Because of her work schedule, she was unable to participate in an educational program about nutrition, one of the requirements for participating in WIC. Therefore, she could not receive WIC benefits.

She also applied to a local utilities assistance program. However, it could provide only limited help. Staff at the utility program interviewed Sarah:

> . . . and they say, "Well, we'll pay $50." My electric bill's $150. So, they'll pay $50, okay. They say, well the resources have gone down so they won't be able to put the amount that they pledged, that they told me on the phone. They'll have to contact me with the amount that they can pledge. Well, sooner or later, the amount that they pledge was like $35. That couldn't do anything to my electric bill; they didn't want to hear that.

Sarah wished the people at the agencies she dealt with could recognize the different problems she faced and understand how complicated her life was.

> Everybody's situation is different. So, I think they lose that point, right there, that everybody's situation is different. You don't have to be rude to me, you know. I'm being very nice and polite, you don't have to be real mean to me. And the same thing with the system, they treat us like "No, no, no, no." Well, computer, hello, the client didn't make the mistake. We [the agency] made

the mistake. So, there should be a way to alter that. You understand what I'm saying, there should be a way to fix it.

In spite of her multiple attempts to get help as summer approached, Sarah still didn't have health insurance. She remained on a waiting list for a subsidized apartment after losing her house nine months earlier, when she could not make her payments. And she depended on friends and relatives for food.

But everything is still chaotic . . . and I'm still waiting on the approval for this house or this apartment, and I don't worry about that much food, because that's the reason why I live from one family to the other.

Even her daily food depended in part on the friends and relatives with whom she stayed.

Focused on her family's daily survival, Sarah had difficulty thinking in terms of long-range plans. Her energies and attention were fully occupied by the pressures and problems associated with keeping her family just hovering on the brink of destitution without plunging into disarray.

The Legacy of Welfare

Because several years have passed since the 1995 Texas welfare reform legislation and the 1996 federal legislation, it is possible to evaluate what these policies have accomplished. Although cash welfare roles have dropped, real changes in the lives of the low-income single mothers and their children most directly affected by the legislative changes are not evident. This book examines the experience of welfare reform in Texas, an experience we believe has not just regional but national ramifications. Despite implementation of a range of policy initiatives designed to change both the behavior of and the outcomes for low-income Texas families, the economic lives of families are much the same as they were at the beginning of welfare reform, with one exception: in the immediate aftermath of welfare reform, these families did not spend as much time on the public dole. However, evidence gathered during the economic downturn of 2000–2002 suggests that even that change may not be permanent (Loprest, 2003).

This book summarizes study findings on families in Texas who left welfare, and their subsequent life experiences. Whether or not the families reverted to welfare, most families whose cash assistance ended undoubtedly continued to live at or below the poverty line. Many of them experienced considerable instability and risk in their daily lives. Sarah's challenges exemplify the three interrelated themes around which this book is organized, themes that define reality for low-income families who left welfare during welfare reform:

- Families stayed poor. Even when Sarah was working, her household remained in poverty. Families leaving TANF were unlikely to move out of poverty even when they found sustained employment, as Sarah did.

- Families faced multiple barriers. Sarah continually battled multiple barriers and problems, although she did not identify herself as a person confronting barriers. Families leaving TANF often struggled with one or more barriers to successful employment.

- Families did not get services. Sarah could not find her way through the bureaucratic maze to obtain the support services for which she was most likely eligible. Even families that appeared eligible for services often failed to successfully negotiate the bureaucratic eligibility process, and many families with demonstrable needs did not qualify for services.

These accounts are presented within a framework of statistics and econometric modeling that draws together administrative data from nine government programs serving low-income families in Texas and a statewide survey of families who left welfare. We identify the policies that worked and were valued by low-income families, as well as those that actually made it harder for poor families, working or unemployed, to improve their everyday circumstances. We also explore the problems and the advantages of welfare reform for a range of families across a variety of settings. The three interrelated themes that characterize the experiences of those who have left welfare since welfare reform emerge vividly in low-income families' stories: their continuing economic insecurity, the numerous problems and barriers they faced in getting assistance and getting on their feet, and their lack of access to a safety net of basic human services.

Economic Insecurity. In Texas, almost all families who left welfare in the period 1998–2000 remained in or near poverty, and nearly half of them remained likely, even when off welfare, to return to the rolls at some time in the future. They struggled with jobs that were close to minimum wage and offered little prospect for advancement. Their jobs were often part-time, with little continuity. Not only did Texas have one of the lowest monthly cash welfare payments in the nation but the eligibility criteria to qualify for welfare were more stringent than in other states. Many families who would have qualified for welfare assistance elsewhere were not eligible to receive it in Texas. Because of these restrictive eligibility criteria, work of any kind usually resulted in a family earning too much money to qualify for welfare benefits; in fact, working many part-time jobs could result in a family becoming ineligible. Consequently, only very poor families were on TANF in Texas in the first place.

On welfare or in a low-wage job, families were still poor. Like Sarah, many of the job holders in families that had left welfare struggled with budgets that barely covered their living expenses. These budgets were viable only as long as the families were receiving some public assistance (such as food stamps or Medicaid) and did not incur additional unexpected expenses. Reductions in received assistance or family emergencies could drive these families into genuine material hardship in which housing was unsettled, nonemergency medical conditions went untreated, and a mother wondered how she would feed her family the following day.

Multiple Problems. About one-third of the families left welfare only to continue to face multiple and compounding barriers to their survival. These families contended with problems that included inadequate medical care, substandard housing, unreliable child care, food insecurity, and a lack of transportation. Together these issues often thwarted the efforts of low-income parents to find and retain jobs and to support their families when they were employed. Furthermore, these problems were interrelated and often exacerbated one another. For example, a family without transportation had limited access to child care; a family in which the children were experiencing health problems in a context of minimal medical care might not be able to afford child care at all. The complexity of these families' daily lives was not reflected in the design of public assistance programs. However, our research illustrates how mothers like Sarah struggled simultaneously with multiple issues of housing loss, irregular child care, and difficulty obtaining medical care, all while working in unstable, low-wage jobs.

Weak Safety Net. Most families who left welfare did not have consistent access to support services as they tried to sustain low-wage employment. Even when transitional benefits were provided, as their time off welfare lengthened, they faced a shortage of affordable and reliable child care options, as was evident from the extensive waiting lists in many areas for subsidized care. Few families leaving welfare can maintain continuous health insurance for all family members for any length of time. Even access to food stamps, the program with the broadest eligibility criteria, was constrained by demands for recertification appointments for eligibility and, for those with older children, work requirements. Sarah's struggles illustrate some of the difficulties mothers faced after welfare in finding and keeping health insurance and needed housing subsidies, as well as in gaining access to other programs that might lift families out of destitution.

Families productively utilized a number of programs in their struggle to secure and keep a job, including subsidized child care, medical care, and housing programs. Large federal programs, such as food stamps and Medicaid, as well as state, local, and municipal programs that provided child care subsidies and transportation assistance, were valued as helpful by families. Despite the popu-

larity of these programs with those who received them, some low-income families remained ineligible for services, and still others believed themselves to be
ineligible because they misunderstood the complex rules controlling access
to support services. Limited program budgets, even for some federal and state
programs, and stringent eligibility requirements were the major constraints
that families experienced, rather than the nature of the services themselves. Although families in poverty faced many barriers, adequately funded public programs, when available, gave families a better chance of finding jobs and keeping
them.

Organization of the Book

The first two chapters of this book set the stage for an examination of life after
welfare in Texas. Sarah's story is similar to the stories of many families who left
TANF and experienced problematic outcomes in terms of work, health insurance,
child care, housing, food and nutrition, and transportation. Her story illustrates
how a working family can be poor, face multiple barriers to achieving stability,
and still receive only limited assistance, even in times of substantial need. In this
book we explore the lives of many other families, sometimes struggling, sometimes succeeding, but almost always at risk of hard times should a job, needed
services, or social supports fail them.

Before exploring the lives of these Texas welfare leavers, we locate these families in the context and history of both national and state welfare policies. In this
chapter we briefly review the history of welfare reform, followed by an overview
of Texas policies. The research methods used in the data collection and analysis
are also discussed.

In the second chapter, we examine trends in poverty, employment, health
insurance, education, and family composition that marked the social and economic context within which low-income families lived and worked in Texas in
the 1999–2001 period of our research. We also explore the ways in which the
experiences of poor Texas families differed from those of other poor families in
the United States, and how trends in Texas can illuminate trends occurring in
the rest of the country. We look specifically at the research sites where we talked
in detail with families who had recently left welfare.

Chapter 3 describes how the weak safety net in Texas affected low-income
families who were struggling to support themselves. Low welfare payments,
complex welfare rules, and unhelpful staff members in local welfare offices all
contributed to this story. Those families that experienced case management
from supportive workers and assistance in applying for programs talked about

the importance of such help. In either case, families struggled to make the transition from welfare to work. Even when employed, they often needed additional help to afford and keep health insurance and other benefits that working parents need to balance their work and family responsibilities.

Chapter 4 examines the extent to which families who left welfare were employed, the patterns of employment they experienced, the types of jobs they were able to find, the wages they earned, and the impact of all these factors on their families. We explore the nature of these jobs in terms of stability, wages, access to benefits, and flexibility. We found that welfare leavers often held jobs with irregular and variable hours, low wages, frequent layoffs, and minimal benefits. They often engaged in repetitive physical work and stood for long hours at a time. We also consider the importance of other nonwelfare income in their lives, in particular income gained through formal child support payments and the Earned Income Tax Credit.

In Chapter 5, we review the barriers that made it difficult for families to leave welfare and obtain steady employment. Although most jobs paid more than Texas welfare, many families leaving welfare had inadequate access to transitional benefits that might have helped them leave TANF; they were struggling with problems in addition to their need for income. These problems included lack of child care, unreliable transportation, and personal health problems. Our respondents also touched on other, less obvious barriers that interfered with their ability to find and keep jobs: their children's and other household members' health problems, food insecurity, and insecure housing. About a third of families we talked to were struggling with several of these problems at the same time.

Chapter 6 examines how some families were able to successfully leave welfare yet still remained vulnerable to subsequent poverty and a return to welfare. Here we use quantitative data to examine statistically which programs were most likely to make a difference in families' lives and which issues created the most pronounced barriers. In particular, we examine those supports and experiences most closely associated with employment and those associated with both departures from and returns to TANF.

Chapter 7 briefly considers how welfare policies have evolved since we talked to the families in our study, and uses the findings from this study to discuss how successful the welfare reform policies are likely to be. In particular, we emphasize the importance of investing in family well-being and the need to address the many barriers low-income families face as they enter the labor force. We argue that these barriers must be addressed simultaneously and the various programs integrated coherently if families are to achieve economic security.

Before journeying into the experience of welfare leavers in Texas, we will set the stage for that trek. Welfare reform itself changed the environment in which impoverished families live. Furthermore, the implementation of welfare reform in Texas was both different from and representative of welfare reform in the rest of the nation.

Welfare Reform: The Nation and Texas

Welfare at the federal level was enacted in 1935 as part of the Social Security Act. Its coverage expanded over the years to include not only impoverished children but an unemployed parent as well (1961). With this and other expansions, the name of the program was changed from Aid to Dependent Children (ADC) to Aid to Families with Dependent Children (AFDC).

Early experiments with welfare were inspired by a series of studies on the dynamics of welfare beginning in the early 1980s (Bane and Ellwood, 1986) that allowed policy-makers to identify factors that appeared to keep people poor. These studies led to a number of welfare-to-work initiatives, including the national Family Support Act of 1988, that tightened work requirements for parents in families receiving welfare. Then, during the 1990s, several states, including Texas, applied for and received waivers from the federal legislation in order to experiment with policies that imposed various restrictions, including time limits, sanctions and penalties, work requirements, and income supplementation.

In 1996, Congress passed the Personal Responsibility and Work Opportunity Reconciliation Act (PRWORA), which established TANF as the replacement for AFDC, the nation's cash assistance program for poor families that had been in place since the mid-1930s. Within general guidelines from the federal government, states were able to develop and adopt their own plans, and they did so, often pursuing somewhat diverse philosophies about what measures were most important. In some areas, strict time limits and requirements were paired with heavy expenditures on education and training. In other states, such as Texas, the emphasis was on reducing the welfare rolls through immediate job placement, if possible, and if not, then through the more punitive measures of denying, discouraging, or financially punishing recipients who did not adhere to all the terms of the state's required personal responsibility agreement.

Unlike the Family Support Act, which was guided by research findings, PRWORA's approach was predicated on theoretical assumptions about the culture of poverty. A leading assumption was that poor people engaged in culturally induced behaviors that led them to be poor and thus had to be changed. The more punitive actions also took a one-size-fits-all approach that assumed that all welfare families needed behavior modification. Such an approach left little room to assist families in overcoming the range of barriers they faced. In fact, many of the ideas that motivated the most recent wave of welfare reform were not empirically tested before being implemented in many states across the country.

One motivation for writing this book was to inform future welfare policy planning through a clearer understanding of what happens to families following policy changes. Changes to the cash assistance program were occurring throughout the period of our study and have continued to the present day. During the course of our study, poor families in Texas were served through the program established by a Texas AFDC waiver (Achieving Change for Texas) that did not expire until 2002, so there were some differences between the Texas system and the federal law. For instance, Texas limited cash assistance to between one and three years for some adults, in addition to the federal lifetime limit of sixty months. In contrast to the federal law, Texas allowed recipients who reached state time limits to return to welfare after not receiving cash assistance for a five-year period. Furthermore, dependent children could continue receiving benefits until a parent reached the federal limits even if the parent no longer received TANF.

Between 1996 and the time of our family interviews and survey in 1999–2001, Texas put into place several other policies. In November and December 1997, the Texas Department of Human Services (DHS) and the Texas Workforce Commission (TWC) instituted Texas Works and a Work First program called Choices, both designed to emphasize to welfare applicants the expectation that they would move on to employment as soon as possible. Texas Works also provided resources designed to divert (or redirect) applicants from welfare into employment even before they had completed a welfare application.

In 1999, the state legislature expanded the Earned Income Disregard: TANF recipients could now disregard 90 percent of up to $1,400 of monthly earnings for four months to maintain continued eligibility for TANF. This was a considerable increase over the previous law's allowance of one-third of their income, but TANF recipients still had incomes below poverty guidelines. Over the period of our interviews, Texas also changed the workforce activity exemption guidelines for parents of very young children, from exempting parents of children less than four years old in 1997 to exempting only parents of children less than two years old in 2000.[1]

As this history indicates, Texas welfare reform was not a single event but a series of policies that were enacted and implemented over time, and the changes and tweaking continued after the period covered by our research. This piecemeal approach to reform contributed to low-income families' confusion about the rules. Not only families but also agency staff had difficulty keeping up with the changes in legislation. Legislative changes had to be translated into regulations and then into training materials for agency staff, who in turn explained the rules to welfare applicants and recipients.

The population of welfare recipients we studied was as complex and variable as welfare reform itself. The welfare leavers who are the focus of this book were also a complicated group composed of many subgroups. Welfare leavers were people who left welfare because they found a job, got married, acquired child support, or received some other type of regular financial assistance. They were people who cycled off and on welfare over a period of years and who, although off welfare at the time of the study, were likely to return. They were also people who found the cash assistance so minimal and the difficulties of complying with welfare regulations so cumbersome that they left the welfare rolls without having another reliable source of income. To fully comprehend the aftermath of welfare reform in poor Texas families' lives, we explore the diversity of family experiences that resulted in families' departure from welfare. Welfare regulations were complicated and included a number of waivers or exceptions to the rules, and they were applied to families with a wide range of experiences, problems, and resources. Families varied not only in their ability to take care of themselves but also in their ability to navigate the welfare bureaucracy. These differences among families are an important part of the story of welfare reform and its effects on families.

Since the expiration of the Texas welfare waiver in 2002, Texas policies toward low-income families on welfare have, with some notable exceptions, become considerably harsher than those in place during the period of our study, 1999–2001. Changes from 2001 on have included full-family sanctions, which remove all family members from welfare if a parent fails to follow increasingly complex rules, and the proposed application of personal responsibility agreement provisions to families receiving Medicaid (a provision since set aside by the courts).[2] Such approaches hold little promise for improving the lives of low-income families. On the contrary, they merely exacerbated families' confusion about how to get assistance during times of greatest crisis and failed to maximize opportunities for families to stabilize themselves. Some changes, such as increased income set-asides (where some income did not count against TANF eligibility), on the other hand, provided valuable and valued support.

Study Population and Methods

The TANF leavers we study here included both single-parent and two-parent families whose TANF cash grant ended for all family members and who did not return to TANF for at least two months. We intentionally excluded the few families who had left TANF because they had reached their state time limits. The difficulties and hardships detailed here were experienced by families who left because they became ineligible, found a different source of income, or were unable or unwilling to meet the requirements for TANF participation. TANF leavers were studied during two time periods: April 1998 to June 1999 (Cohort 1) and July to September 2000 (Cohort 2).

We used three research methods to explore the lives of families leaving TANF. Our demographic and longitudinal analysis used administrative data files, intensive interviews, and econometric regressions to study Cohort 1 TANF leavers. For our analysis of Cohort 2 TANF leavers, we conducted demographic and longitudinal analyses of administrative data, a statewide survey, and econometric regressions. We were able to follow the earlier cohort for a full year after the families' departure from TANF, and the later cohort for three months. We present data from either of the two cohorts, depending on which question we are addressing and whether the two cohorts behaved differently from each other.

First, the project team worked to link together individual-level administrative data files from programs that serve low-income families. This combined data set allowed us to determine the demographic characteristics marking different groups of welfare users and leavers. The data also allowed us to follow families' participation in TANF and other programs that served low-income families over time. A number of state agencies contributed data, including the Texas Workforce Commission and the Texas DHS, both of which managed important aspects of the welfare program, as well as agencies that collected child support, investigated reports of child abuse or neglect, or placed children in foster care. We refer to this source of information as the administrative data set.

Second, in what we refer to as the phone-mail survey, we collected information from 723 members of a random sample of 1,596 families who left TANF in September 2000 and remained off TANF for at least two months. We surveyed these families approximately six months after they had left TANF. We were able to confirm that 581 of the original sample of 1,596 families had moved and were no longer available at the address where we tried to contact them. Poor families in Texas experience a great deal of mobility. Rural families often move to follow agricultural work, while urban families move to find less expensive rent and to take advantage of the support of friends and family during periods of homelessness. We mailed a survey to all families, with follow-up telephone calls to reach as many families as possible. A follow-up survey was sent to all deliverable addresses. In the course of all of this activity, we learned not only about family geographic mobility (the primary reason why we failed to reach families) but also about families where the mother was dead, in the hospital, or in jail, or where the mother worked so many hours that she could not be reached in our follow-up effort.

Third, we interviewed in person welfare leavers in two large metropolitan areas (Bexar County, which includes San Antonio, and Harris County, which includes Houston), one smaller city area (McLennon County, which includes Waco), and three more rural areas (Jasper County in East Texas, Hale County in the Texas Panhandle, and Cameron and Hidalgo Counties on the Texas-Mexico border). These interviews provided examples of the workings of welfare policies in families' lives. They let us probe into the different types of experiences that arose as families dealt with poverty, employment, welfare, and a range of other life factors in widely varying locales.

In this book we use all three kinds of data—the administrative files, the phone-mail survey, and personal interviews—to develop a picture of the workings of welfare reform in Texas during the late 1990s. In particular, we have combined the survey data with the administrative data available on our research families. We were particularly interested in understanding the relative weight of different factors—participation in welfare programs, access to medical insurance, use of subsidized child care, access to other child care, medical conditions, and a range of other family issues—associated with families' successful employment or return to welfare.

Most poor people in Texas did not receive cash welfare. Of those who were on welfare, not all left. Thus, the welfare leavers themselves, while a large group, represent a special set of low-income families. Ninety-four percent of Texas families who left TANF during the 1999–2001 period of our study were headed by single women. Nearly 40 percent of these parents were less than twenty-five years old, while another third were between twenty-six and thirty-four years old. Nearly half (45 percent) were Hispanic, with the remainder divided somewhat evenly between Black and white caretakers. Most families had two children, with the youngest child less than five years old. Only half of the caretakers had completed high school. To the degree we were able to confirm it, people who responded to the mail survey and people whom we interviewed in the six sites matched the demographic characteristics of the general population of families who left the cash welfare rolls during this period.

Earlier research also set the stage for this study. The primary authors, Laura Lein and Deanna Schexnayder, have worked on poverty issues for two decades, and the book is also informed by our other work. Indeed, part of this story is decades old. In Texas, challenges for the working poor have always been present, against the backdrop of somewhat ephemeral services provided by welfare. Poverty is a problem for those employed in low-wage jobs as well as for those dependent on welfare over the long term (Schexnayder et al., 1991). In Texas as elsewhere, low welfare benefit levels in combination with families' desire to work tends to produce family patterns of cycling between welfare and low-wage work (Schexnayder et al., 1998). Low educational levels and other barriers faced by many low-income families often inhibit these families' ability to earn high enough wages in the unskilled labor market to successfully leave poverty, a pattern largely unchanged by recent welfare reforms (Schexnayder, Lein, et al., 2002; Schexnayder, Schroeder, et al., 2002). Families continue to find it difficult to support themselves by working in the jobs currently available to them.

Earlier work (Edin and Lein, 1997) also showed the degree to which families elsewhere in the nation shared some of the problems and barriers to stability experienced by impoverished families in Texas, even before welfare reform, as well as more recent work following welfare reform (Loprest, 2002; Moffitt et al., 2002; Zedlewski, 2002). Families could not really make it financially either on welfare or on the wages they received in the jobs that were most likely to follow welfare. They often experienced periods of material hardship with little access to medical insurance, child care, or secure housing.

Research in several states has arrived at different conclusions concerning the experiences of welfare leavers. In a recent study, Danziger et al. (2002; see also Cawley and Danziger, 2005), who used Michigan data, demonstrated that welfare leavers do better economically once they have left welfare and moved into wage dependence. These findings were contradicted in part by Moffit and Winder (2005), who used data from three states—Massachusetts, Illinois, and Texas—to show that a large part of the increase in financial well-being comes from contributions from others. Although debate over such issues is ongoing, most researchers agree that welfare leavers are not likely to emerge from poverty in the years immediately after they leave the welfare rolls (Baj et al., 2001; King and Mueser, 2005; King et al., 1991).

The experience in Texas is illuminating not just for Texas state policy-makers and citizens but for the entire country. Although the Three-City Study (on which Moffitt drew) and studies pertaining to other states (Isaacs and Lyon, 2000) indicate differences among states in the aftermath of welfare reform, almost all studies agree that welfare leavers generally remain in poverty. In this context, and in a time of government financial retrenchment, Texas represents an interesting and important case. For the population of Texas reflects the diversity of the United States as a whole. Welfare leavers, like welfare recipients, include people of all races and ethnicities. They have various levels of education and deal with different medical conditions and family responsibilities. All of these factors make a difference in why they need welfare in the first place and what their prospects are as they leave welfare.

Welfare reform policies are experienced differently by the diverse groups of

people living in the wide-ranging parts of Texas' geographic, social, and economic landscape. The size and diversity of Texas allow us to explore the experiences of individuals on welfare in both urban and rural settings, among people
who live in one-employer communities and people who experience the opportunities and problems found in large metropolitan settings with many employers.
Within this state's expanse, important climatic variations exist, ranging from settings where summer air conditioning is a necessity for many people's continuing
good health to areas where winter days without heat can be deadly. People live
both in sparsely populated areas with limited access to medical care available
and in dense urban centers near world-renowned teaching and research hos-
pitals. All of these differences, and many more, form the diversity of settings
within which impoverished families live after welfare.

TWO

The Context for Texas Poverty and Welfare

FAMILIES LIVING IN poverty in Texas experienced different degrees of poverty, which were conditioned in part by the human welfare policies in the state and the history of those welfare policies. Their experiences were also conditioned by the local environment—geophysical, social, and economic—as is evident in the descriptions of the areas where we interviewed welfare leavers. After discussing the effect of changing regulations and the local environment on the experience of poverty, we take a broad look at the social and economic demography of Texas, including trends in the overall composition of the poverty population, family structure, employment, and education. We end the chapter by outlining the social welfare programs that most directly affect the lives of impoverished families.

Although the Temporary Assistance to Needy Families (TANF) program serves Texas families in different geographic areas and in different areas of need to varying effect, the overarching philosophy of Texas welfare reform is summed up in the words of a state agency publication: "Independence has long been a word associated with Texas, and today it applies to a growing number of Texans." According to that publication, the goal of the program is to ensure that "the pride of self-sufficiency replaces the mindset of entitlement" (Texas Department of Human Services [DHS], 2000).[1]

According to the rationale for welfare reform, welfare programs exist to help families move successfully along a path from welfare to self-sufficiency. We briefly summarize the extent to which such programs in the crucial areas of health insurance, food and housing assistance, child care, and cash assistance are available to eligible Texas families. We examine how families' access to welfare differs in different areas of Texas and by specific region. We begin by exploring the different areas where the welfare leavers we interviewed lived.

Poverty in Different Parts of Texas

By interviewing families in six different parts of Texas, we saw how the lives of low-income families who had left welfare varied from one area to another, as well as the ways in which the experience of poverty was the same across the state.[2] Like any other large state, Texas comprises a number of more localized economies and populations. Each of the six areas we visited—Harris County, Bexar County, McLennan County, Cameron and Hidalgo Counties, Hale County, and Jasper County—provided a different perspective on post-welfare life for low-income families. We visited and worked in each of these communities between July and December 1999 (Figure 2.1).

Harris County

Harris County includes the state's largest city, Houston. With 3,400,578 residents in 2000, the county was home to almost a sixth of the state's population. Houston is an oil and manufacturing center, as well as an international seaport. As an active tourist site, it also draws convention business into the local economy. Despite its varied economy, 15 percent of Harris County's large population had an income below the poverty line (and the child poverty rate was 20 percent); thus, this area accounted for a substantial fraction of the state's welfare rolls. As a large, urban, metropolitan area, Houston, and more generally Harris County, exhibited considerable racial and ethnic diversity: 33 percent of the county residents were Hispanic, 19 percent were Black, and 5 percent were classified as Asian.

In Houston itself, the families we interviewed faced difficulties related to urban living. Like residents of other impoverished urban areas, families had to contend with neighborhood crime and the drug trade, poor city services, and overcrowded housing. Despite the extensive highway system and a large public transportation system, families reported difficulties in getting around the city, and our Harris County interviewers experienced these problems firsthand. Families with jobs in distant parts of the city and children in care at different

FIGURE 2.1. Map of Texas counties showing sites of research and interviews with informants.

locations might spend hours every day on the bus because of the long distances traveled and the high density of rush-hour traffic.

Some low-income families lived in large public housing projects; others lived in equally anonymous low-rent apartment buildings. Throughout our interviews there, we were struck by how isolated many families were in their own communities. Often a family we were looking for had moved and the neighbors did not know where they had gone, and the building management had no forwarding address or phone number. In some cases, neighbors were not even aware the family had moved.

Bexar County

Bexar County also includes a large metropolitan area. Located on Highway IH-35, which runs down through the central United States into Mexico, this county is dominated by the city of San Antonio. In 2000 the county's population was 1,392,931. Bexar County had high rates of poverty, with a 16 percent overall poverty rate and a child poverty rate of 22 percent. The high poverty rates have in part resulted from depressed wages owing both to the ongoing loss of manufacturing jobs from the San Antonio economy and to the increasing pool of immigrant workers. Bexar County had lost manufacturing jobs in a variety of industries, from clothing manufacturing to meatpacking—industries in which the TANF leavers might otherwise have hoped to obtain jobs. In contrast, San Antonio's tourism and regional health care industries remained substantial. However, the tourism and health care jobs available to unskilled workers were often seasonal and entailed irregular hours and shifting schedules. The county population was more than half Hispanic (54 percent), with a 7 percent Black population.

Many Bexar County families that participated in the study lived in large, one- and two-story public housing projects that occupied hundreds of acres and included some of the oldest public housing in the country. According to the neighborhood lore, Eleanor Roosevelt as first lady attended the opening of one such project. The quality of housing varied enormously. Some public housing had been recently renovated, with larger units, fresh flooring and paint, and new bathroom fixtures. Other units appeared almost untouched since the 1930s and exhibited cracks, broken fixtures, and an active rodent and insect population.

A number of policy experiments and innovations occurred in San Antonio under the rubric of welfare reform. Under the Achieving Change for Texas (ACT) waiver in effect during the time of our interviews with residents, many families had been assigned to different experimental groups, each with different time limits for benefits, work requirements, and access to services. In addition, some San Antonio families were also served by smaller educational and training programs operated by nongovernment organizations with their own guidelines and procedures. As a result, both interviewers and the families they talked with often found it difficult to understand the policy variations in San Antonio.

McLennan County

McLennan County, which includes the city of Waco, is in central Texas, about 100 miles north of the Texas capital of Austin. A medium-size urban area, the county had a population of 213,517 in 2000. Although primarily urban, the county also includes agricultural and rural communities. In 2000 the county's population was primarily white, with a 15 percent Black representation and an 18 percent Hispanic representation. The overall poverty rate was 18 percent and the child poverty rate was 21 percent. Located along the "NAFTA Superhighway" corridor of IH-35, 180 miles north of San Antonio, Waco and McLennan County were often described as experiencing economic growth. Although some families we interviewed were living in conditions of rural poverty, others seemed to be progressing economically, often as a result of the education and training programs available to them.

McLennan County was, in fact, the beneficiary of a private sector grant that supported the development of innovative education and training programs for some of the welfare population. We met more families in McLennan County participating in education and training programs than in any other site in the study. Almost uniformly, these program participants highly valued their educational and training experiences. Although relatively few people who were enrolled in such programs had completed their education and entered employment at the time of our interviews, a number of them were looking forward with optimism to the jobs for which they were training. Even in the relatively small city of Waco, however, education and training programs reached only a small number of those leaving TANF. Many people, particularly those living in the more rural areas, knew little about these opportunities or how to take advantage of them.

Cameron and Hidalgo Counties

Cameron and Hidalgo Counties together occupy the extreme southern tip of Texas, with populations of 371,825 and 569,463 respectively. (The counties are treated together here because they have similar economic and demographic profiles.) Urban centers in these counties include Brownsville, Harlingen, McAllen, and Edinburgh. The population was more than 80 percent Hispanic (84 percent for Cameron County and 88 percent for Hidalgo County) and less than 1 percent Black. Located in the Rio Grande Valley, which forms the border with Mexico, the region was characterized by high unemployment and poverty rates, with about a third of the population living below the poverty line (33 percent and 36 percent, respectively) and with child poverty rates in excess of 40 percent (43 percent and 46 percent). Although these counties have medium-size urban centers, agriculture still figured heavily in the local economies, as did tourism and seafood processing. Largely because of the North American Free Trade Agreement (NAFTA), manufacturing had been growing in importance in the region. By the end of

1996, there were 2,411 *maquiladora* factories (up from 2,114 in 1993) in the border cities from Matamoros to El Paso/Juarez, but primarily on the Mexican side of the border (The number continued climbing to 2,882 in 2001, according to the Instituto Nacional de Estadística, Geografía e Informática in Mexico.)

Many Mexican and Mexican-American families on both sides of the border lived in *colonias,* unincorporated communities where many families build and own their own housing. Families in these communities often experienced substandard housing, a lack of utilities, and minimal public services. Roads were unpaved, and sewage and drainage were primitive. In some cases, our research staff waited for days to enter a colonia that had been flooded out, an occurrence that was not uncommon, according to colonia residents. *La Migra,* the border patrol, was powerful and visible in the lives of families, even those families who were legal immigrants or residents. Families frequently told us of their fears of being stopped, questioned, held, or deported.

While agricultural work opportunities attracted workers on both sides of the border, the United States was also engaged in continuing efforts to tighten the border. Both our student interviewers and the families we interviewed were anxious about border crossings. Our research team, which included several international students, experienced this firsthand when they were questioned at the border following occasional day trips or evening excursions into Mexico.

Hale County

Hale County, in the Texas Panhandle, had a total population of about 36,602 in 2000, with its county seat dominating the county. The county is an agricultural center in the northern part of Texas. During our time in Hale, the cotton gins were active, and the meatpacking plant was also hiring. However, neither plant offered job security—the cotton gins operated only two months out of the year, and the meatpacking work was also somewhat seasonal, in addition to being physically arduous. Workers we interviewed often did not know whether and where they would be working the following month. Hale had a large Hispanic population—48 percent of the county, with a much smaller Black population of only 6 percent. Overall, the county had a poverty rate of 18 percent and a child poverty rate of 23 percent.

Agricultural workers tended to live in low-rent rural housing. Although some families we interviewed had jobs in the cotton gins and other agriculturally based businesses, others worked in the fields for low and irregular wages. Some public housing was available.

The county police forces kept a close eye on outsiders. Members of our re-

search team were stopped several times, even after we had visited the police sta-
tion and introduced ourselves. One of the few large public housing projects "in
town" had a curfew for young people; those under eighteen leaving or entering
the project between 10:00 p.m. and 7:00 a.m. were questioned by a police officer
stationed at the entrance.

We worked in Hale County just before Thanksgiving. This was a period when
harvesting work was coming to an end, but the associated work of ginning cotton and processing other harvests continued. Some migrant workers were still
in the area, but overall, employment prospects in the area were shrinking as
November ended.

Jasper County

Jasper County, the most sparsely populated of the sites we visited, had a county-
wide population of 35,604. The largest town, Jasper, accounted for about 20 percent of the county population. Jasper County had a poverty rate of 18 percent
and a child poverty rate of 23 percent.

Located in the heart of East Texas, Jasper County's major industries reflected
those of the larger region and were primarily related to timber and oil. In Jasper,
agricultural work in the forests had a distinctive rhythm. Trees are not harvested
on an annual basis, and foresting jobs were often irregular. Consequently, jobs
in the small manufacturing plants and in fast food outlets were prized, since
most agricultural workers could not attain a similar level of stability. Although
few welfare leavers received them, some of the most desirable and stable jobs
could be found working for the recently built state prison. Jasper had a significant Black population (18 percent,) with only a small number of Hispanics
(4 percent). As in many rural counties, only limited medical services and child
care services were available, and there was no public transportation. There were
several public housing projects, but many impoverished families lived in trailer
parks or in relatively isolated substandard homes outside the town of Jasper.

Many rural low-income families in Jasper were able to subsist in part by
hunting for squirrels and maintaining small gardens. Some family homes had
no inside plumbing or cooking facilities, so that families instead relied on out-
houses and outdoor cooking fires. Few community-based resources existed to
help families in trouble when they faced evictions, food shortages, sudden medical crises, or other emergencies. One family, more isolated than most, called our
800 number requesting an immediate interview. After losing their housing, this
two-parent family was living in a room provided by the Red Cross. Not knowing
how they would feed their children the next day, they were desperate for the

grocery store gift certificate that families received when they participated in our research.

We interviewed families in Jasper between September 24, 1999, and October 16, 1999, a significant time in Jasper's racial history. One year earlier, in an incident that drew national attention, a local African-American man had been dragged to death behind a pickup truck on a country road in Jasper. Our interviews occurred in the period between the second and third trials of the perpetrators. While many people described the murder as an aberration perpetrated by "outsiders," Black parents in Jasper with whom we talked were vigilant in their care of sons and daughters, whom they watched closely and tried to keep inside at night.

Economic and Demographic Overview of Texas

Although the families interviewed in this study lived in a variety of communities, they all contributed to the state's overall economic, demographic, and social characteristics. We briefly review that overall context to provide a snapshot of the Texas population and economy, as well as the level of the state's current investment in education and social programs.

Texas Population Composition and Trends

Throughout its history, the state of Texas has experienced more rapid growth than the rest of the United States.[3] In 2000, the total Texas population exceeded 20 million, making it the second most populous state in the nation. In the decade of 1990–2000 alone, the Texas population increased by 3.8 million. The population growth during this period was almost equally divided between a natural increase in the ratio of births to deaths and a net migration to Texas from other states and countries.

Although all parts of the state experienced growth, metropolitan counties accounted for more than 90 percent of the state's population growth over the past decade. Indeed, contrary to popular perception, most Texans live in metropolitan areas, and three of the ten largest cities in the nation—Houston, Dallas, and San Antonio—are in Texas. In the year 2000, 67 percent of all Texans lived in central city counties, 18 percent lived in suburban counties, and only 15 percent lived in rural areas. The fastest-growing regions of the state during the past decade were areas along the Texas-Mexico border, in the central corridor from Dallas–Fort Worth through San Antonio, and the Houston-Galveston area.

In addition to growing rapidly, the population of Texas has become more diverse over time. Over the last twenty years, the nonwhite portions of the population and the Hispanic population have grown more rapidly than the white population. By 2000, the overall population was 53 percent non-Hispanic white, 32 percent Hispanic, and 12 percent Black. The state demographer estimates that less than half of all Texans will be white by 2010 (Murdock et al., 2002).

Like the rest of the United States, Texas is aging. However, with a median age of 32.3 in 2000, Texans were still younger than the United States population as a whole. This lower median age is largely accounted for by the rapidly growing share of Hispanics and the young median age of that population group. Sixty percent of Texans under six years old are Hispanic, and 57 percent of all children under eighteen are nonwhite.

The Texas context contributes to the difficulties families face in trying to move off welfare. Although similar in many ways to other southern states, some of the distinctive Texas features forecast problems that may soon emerge in other parts of the country. The poverty rate in Texas in 2000 was above 15 percent, which is 25 percent higher than the national average of approximately 12 percent. These figures place approximately 3,000,000 Texans in poverty. Roughly 20 percent of children in Texas live in poverty, also 25 percent higher than the national average of 16 percent. The South Central region of the United States, with Texas in the middle, lies at the intersection of several national poverty concentrations that include rural and urban poverty, and the full range of racial and ethnic poverty experiences encompasses several different poverty groups in the South and the Southwest. East Texas (including Jasper) features a rural Black population similar in many ways to that of other southern states. Like New Mexico, Arizona, and California, Texas has a large and rapidly growing Hispanic population, particularly evident in the border counties (such as Cameron and Hidalgo Counties, with more than 80 percent Hispanic populations) and San Antonio, one of the first major cities to become more than half Hispanic. Texas has both large pockets of inner-city poverty (as in Houston), with large numbers of African-Americans, Hispanics, and others, and widespread areas of rural poverty (such as are found in Jasper and Hale Counties).

MARRIED COUPLES IN POVERTY

Although poverty is increasingly concentrated among single-parent families in the nation as a whole, Texas also has a large number of two-parent families who live in poverty. In Texas in 2000, roughly 13 percent of two-parent families with children lived in poverty. Individuals in these families represented 46 percent of the total poverty population in the state (Texas Health and Human Services Commission, 2000).

POOR AND WORKING

Most poor adults in Texas are working poor. This group of families remains impoverished even though employed. In the mid-1990s, 15.6 percent of working Texan families were living in poverty, compared to a national percentage of 11.5 percent. Almost half (42 percent) of the impoverished working parents were dependent on service sector wages (Center for Public Policy Priorities, 1999).

HISPANIC AND IMMIGRANT POPULATION

Texas has the second largest Hispanic population in the United States, behind only California. The Hispanic population in Texas has a relatively high employment rate, low household income, and a high birth rate. As a group, Hispanics in Texas are also more likely to be married than other ethnic groups, contributing to the relatively high numbers of married couples in poverty. Unlike other population groups, neither employment nor marriage seems to provide particularly strong protection against poverty for Hispanics living in Texas.

Although some immigrants succeed economically, many do not (Smith and Edmonston, 1997). During the 1980s and 1990s, the number of poor immigrant-headed households nationwide nearly tripled, increasing from 2.7 million to 7.7 million (Camarota, 2001), and the economic situation among immigrants declined (Borjas, 2000). Immigrants made up about 12 percent of America's workforce yet accounted for approximately one-third of the high school dropout rate (Perez, 2000). Immigrants with relatively low levels of education were 60 percent more likely than native-born workers to be employed in low-skilled occupations (Fix and Passel, 1994) and to have fewer assets and less income as they approached retirement (Santos and Seitz, 2000). Mexican, Central American, and Asian immigrants, especially the immigrant elderly, drew on public assistance at higher rates than other immigrant groups (Angel et al., 2006; Bean et al., 1997; Fix and Passel, 1999; Tienda and Jensen, 1986; Trejo, 1992; Van Hook, 2000; Van Hook and Bean, 1998).

The Texas Economy

Historically, the Texas economy has differed significantly from the national economy because of its reliance on oil and gas, agriculture, and the extraction of other natural resources.[4] However, in more recent years, the Texas economy has shifted to more closely resemble the larger U.S. economy, mirroring the same economic trends. These trends include the decline of the manufacturing sector and the accompanying rise of the service sector as the country's largest employers; the growth of a more marginal labor force reliant on temporary or seasonal positions; the globalization of employment across national borders; and a decade-long period of economic expansion throughout the 1990s, followed by an economic downturn, increased unemployment, and a slow recovery in the early 2000s.

At the time of our study, from 1999 to early 2001, the Texas economy, along with the rest of the country, was at the tail end of an economic boom. The overall state unemployment rate in 2000 was 4.4 percent; by early 2002, it had risen to more than 6 percent. However, the overall state unemployment rate masks wide variations in regional unemployment rates across the state. For example, in November 2001, unemployment rates published by the Texas Workforce Commission ranged from a low of 0.8 percent in Collingsworth County in the Texas Panhandle to highs of 19.9 percent to 23.7 percent in Presidio, Staff, and Maverick Counties, near the border with Mexico.

AVAILABLE JOBS

In March 2000, more than a quarter of all jobs in Texas were in the service sector. Other significant sources of jobs were retail trade (18 percent), manufacturing (12 percent), and local government (11 percent). According to some analysts, the current workforce development system has not kept pace with the "new economy" (Cappelli et al., 1997; International Labour Office, 1998), which brings with it higher expectations for education and training (National Governors Association, 2000). Large-scale forces affecting the world's economies include technological advances, increased globalization, new management practices and forms of work organization, and new business practices, such as pursuing niche markets and smaller, more flexible production runs. Demographic shifts are also affecting the Texas and U.S. workforce as the baby-boom generation ages, immigration (both legal and illegal) continues to grow, and the diversity of the workforce expands, with greater participation from women and minorities (Judy and D'Amico, 1997). Public mores and expectations have also been changing in ways that have implications for the U.S. workforce and related policies. Among these changes are greater public support for work over welfare, a stress on individual and personal responsibility, and a greater reliance on market mechanisms rather than on the state or institutional mechanisms for alleviating poverty.

EDUCATION AND IMPLICATIONS FOR THE ECONOMY

Over the past several years, Texas has been surpassed by other states in national rankings on educational measures. In 2000, around the time this research was conducted, Texas ranked forty-fourth among all the states in the share of adults more than twenty-five years old who had graduated from high school. Only three years later, in 2003, Texas ranked last among states on this measure. A Census Bureau survey conducted in 2003 estimated that only 76 percent of Texas adults had completed high school, compared with 85 percent for the United States as a whole. These lower rates of education are related in large part to the rapidly growing Hispanic population in Texas, which is disproportionately lower in its high school graduation rates compared with other groups. When analyzed by race and ethnicity, Texas is second among the six largest states in the United States in high school completion rates for whites and Blacks, but last for Hispanics (McMillon et al., 2005; U.S. Census, 2003 ["Educational Attainment"]).

In general, younger citizens tend to be better educated than their older counterparts, so that the overall education rates of the population can be expected to increase over time. Even though graduation rates are increasing, however, at this point only 66 percent of freshmen entering Texas high schools are expected to complete high school in four years (Urban Institute, 2001a). As economic forecasters and policy-makers warn, adults with lower educational levels are less likely to succeed in the labor force and more likely to need public benefits. In fact, poor educational attainment is often related to a return to welfare after unstable employment experiences.

Social Policies in Texas

In 1999, the per capita income in Texas was $26,525, putting Texas twenty-seventh among all states in the United States (U.S. Census, 2000 ["Quick Facts"]). Even so, Texas typically ranked near the bottom in its expenditures on social programs. In fiscal year 1998, just prior to the beginning of our study, Texas' total per capita welfare expenditures of $548.25 ranked forty-first in the nation (U.S. House of Representatives, 2002). Texas ranked near the bottom of all states on expenditures on health care, food assistance, child care subsidies, and housing programs, the types of assistance on which low-income families rely. Texas families experience need in several areas, and the nature of the help available in each of these areas is not uniform across the state.

WORKFORCE PROGRAMS FOR WELFARE RECIPIENTS

Historically, public workforce programs have been criticized as difficult to understand, sometimes duplicative, and hard to access (U.S. Government Accounting Organization, 1995). These problems are especially relevant for workers and their families in the southwestern United States. In Texas as well as in other states in the region, the difficult life situations and persistent poverty of the working poor have always presented a social and economic challenge equal to that of long-term welfare dependence (Schexnayder et al., 1991). Low welfare benefit levels combined with families' real desire to work have typically produced patterns of cycling between welfare and low-wage work for Texas welfare recipients (Schexnayder et al., 1998). In the changing labor market, low educational levels and other barriers faced by low-income families often keep families from earning their way out of poverty. Unfortunately, this pattern has remained largely unchanged by recent welfare reforms (Schexnayder, Schroeder, et al., 2002).

HEALTH CARE

For several years, Texas has led the nation in having the highest proportion of individuals without health insurance, 21.5 percent (U.S. Census, 2000:Table HI-4). Individuals in this category are not covered either by public programs, such as Medicaid and Medicare, or by private or employer-assisted health insurance. Furthermore, just as families may cycle in and out of the workforce, they also cycle in and out of medical coverage (Angel et al., 2001). Thus, a much greater proportion of individuals spend part of their lives without health insurance than the rate for any given year would indicate.

According to figures from the U.S. Census Bureau, the rate of uninsured children in Texas, 14.7 percent, is twice the U.S. average of 7.3 percent. At the time this study was under way, the state was implementing program changes to benefit the most needy children through the Children's Health Insurance Program (CHIP). Texas began providing services for children under CHIP in May 2000 and had enrolled roughly 600,000 eligible children two years later through a massive recruitment effort that included public service announcements (Shenkman et al., 2002). However, in 2003 the Texas legislature, facing budget shortfalls, significantly cut back on both Medicaid and CHIP coverage. Other studies have corroborated the weakness of the Texas Medicaid system relative to that in other states. The Three City Study showed that only 64 percent of children in families with incomes below the poverty level in San Antonio were enrolled in Medicaid, compared with 82 percent in both Boston and Chicago (Angel et al., 2001).

In addition to the significant gaps in Medicaid coverage for low-income families, Texas, like other south-central states and rural states, has a large number of medically underserved counties, with insufficient numbers of doctors and medical facilities per capita. Families in our study described the difficulties they had getting access to medical services even with medical insurance coverage. Unfortunately, this combination of limited services and erratic medical insurance coverage brought about the situation in which many Texans struggled with untreated medical conditions. In Hale County, low-income workers and migrant farm worker populations in particular were underserved. Even in the two urban sites, Harris and Bexar Counties, large areas within each county were medically underserved. Cameron County was partially underserved, and the entire population and area of Hidalgo County were underserved. In Jasper County, the poverty population throughout the county was underserved. Some areas of McLennon County were underserved (Texas Department of Health, 2002).

CHILD CARE

Most mothers of young children now work outside the home, regardless of their family situation. In 2001, 64 percent of all women in the United States with children less than six years old were in the labor force. The share of employed single-parent mothers with young children is typically higher than the rates for mothers in married-couple families, 67 percent, versus 59 percent in 2001. In recent years, even as the labor force participation rate of married women with young children has dropped slightly, that for single mothers has risen (U.S. Department of Labor, 2003).

As policies for low-income families, particularly low-income mothers with small children, have shifted from welfare to an emphasis on work, subsidized child care programs have increased in importance. The Child Care and Development Fund is the primary source of federal child care assistance for low- and moderate-income families. Despite a dramatic growth in subsidized child care in the years following welfare reform, subsidized child care nationally still reaches only 28 percent of children who are eligible for assistance, leaving many families without care. Waiting lists for families needing care for the purpose of employment remain long (Meyers et al., 2002), and many families we heard from relied on informal and intermittent care provided by relatives and neighbors during their work hours.

In Texas, only a small fraction of eligible children receive subsidized child care. Texas enrolls less than 10 percent of potentially eligible children in subsidized child care, one of the lowest rates among all the states (Collins et al., 2000; Schexnayder et al., 1999). Other studies confirm that mothers without access to more regular child care resort to informal arrangements, which may not always be of the best quality or reliability, to obtain some supervision for their children (Chase-Lansdale et al., 2002).

FOOD AND HOUSING ASSISTANCE

The food stamp program is a central component of the federal government's policy to alleviate hunger and poverty. In fiscal year 2001, nationwide, approximately 60 percent of those eligible for food stamps received them. However, participation rates varied widely from state to state. For example, only 40 to 50 percent of eligible residents of Massachusetts participated in the state's food stamp program, compared with 82 to 96 percent of those eligible in West Virginia. Only 45 to 52 percent of eligible Texans received food stamps around the time of our study (1999–2001). Thus, Texas ranked forty-seventh among all the states (Mathematica Policy Research, 2002).

Subsidized housing assistance programs funded by the U.S. Department of Housing and Urban Development (HUD) typically required participating households to pay rent equal to 30 percent of their income, with the rest paid by the federal government. However, this assistance was available only for a small proportion of eligible families. In 1999, HUD classified nearly five million unassisted renter households across the nation as having "worst need" for rental assistance. At that time, more than 14 percent of all renters fell into this category of housing need (U.S. HUD, 2000). The situation was particularly severe in Texas, where, in 1997, less than one subsidized housing unit existed for every five eligible households (Texas Low Income Housing Information Service, n.d.).

TANF CASH ASSISTANCE

From 1995, when welfare reform efforts began in earnest, until 1999, when the interviews yielding the experiential data recounted in this book were collected, welfare rolls in Texas, as in most parts of the country, dropped dramatically. Throughout this era of welfare reform, the maximum cash transfer to a Texas family of three never exceeded $208 per month. Although fulfilling its obligations under federally mandated programs such as Medicaid and food stamps, Texas has done little to increase either the amount of or accessibility to these benefit programs. Texas remains among the ten lowest-paying states in the country in cash welfare assistance. Both detailed studies of family budgets (Edin and Lein, 1997) and larger-scale analyses of family need (Center for Public Policy Priorities, 2003; Schexnayder et al., 2006) indicate that even the most conservative family budgets are not covered by the amount of the welfare cash transfer, and in low-payment states like Texas, families cannot subsist even when food stamps and housing subsidies are included. In contrast to Texas, states with higher payment levels also have more lenient income and asset eligibility guidelines. In other words, if you live in Texas, you must be poorer than in most states to qualify for TANF benefits. And even small increases in income may result in the loss of benefits. Thus, impoverished Texas families are more likely to cycle on and off welfare than are families in other states. Families in higher-payment states are able to earn more before they reach the threshold for ineligibility. Consequently, they can stay on welfare even while going through unstable periods of employment, and they are able to combine earned income and welfare benefits for longer than families who live in a low-benefit state.

EARNED INCOME TAX CREDIT

The Earned Income Tax Credit (EITC) was introduced by the Clinton administration as part of a welfare reform effort to allow working poor families to gain more income from their work effort than they could directly from their earned wages. Since this credit was expanded in 1996, the value of working poor families' earnings has been enhanced considerably. To receive this credit, families must file a federal tax return even if they do not owe taxes. For the 2000 tax year, people working full-time at minimum wage ($10,300) were eligible for $3,888 from the EITC. A family of three earning at the poverty level could receive as much as $3,684, although unfortunately, not all eligible families know about the tax credit, and only a small percentage apply. According to the Urban Institute's National Survey of America's Families, conducted in 1999, 74 percent of current and 84 percent of past Texas welfare recipients had heard of the EITC. Despite widespread knowledge about the credit, only 33 percent of current and 69 percent of past welfare recipients reported ever receiving the EITC. Almost all families who receive money through the EITC get it in a lump sum when they file their tax returns rather than as a monthly income supplement.

Texas and Welfare Reform: Where Do We Go from Here?

Texas continues to be a state with limited investment in social policy expenditures. Among other indicators, the cash payments to families on welfare have always been among the lowest in the country. Given its history of limited investment in social programs, Texas provides an excellent case study of likely results if the trend to limit services for impoverished families continues in Texas and spreads among states. Although states vary considerably in their expenditures on welfare programs, the federal government is curtailing welfare expenditures, and states, whether or not they have previously cut programs dramatically, are faced with difficult expenditure decisions.

In the context of national welfare reform, then, the Texas experience provides an important venue for the study of the aftermath of welfare reform. Texas is a large state, with a heavily minority impoverished population, that launched an early statewide welfare reform experiment before the national law was enacted. Because national trends include an increasing proportion of ethnic minorities and many states are debating the adoption of more stringent welfare policies, the experience in Texas emerges as an important case study and early example of a potential trend, the application of somewhat punitive and restrictive policies to a large and diverse population. In removing families from welfare, Texas concentrated on low-investment strategies, offering short-term transition and job placement services but little in the way of long-term training and on-the-job support.

In the face of this lack of investment, impoverished families in Texas, particularly those who are not receiving welfare, remain in poverty with the continued prospect of possibly returning to welfare. Not all states have adopted a policy of minimum investment; however, in many states continuing budgetary problems threaten the more expensive programs in place.

As Texas welfare leavers exit TANF, many search for employment and sustainable income. Some leave welfare only to become dependent on another public system, such as Supplemental Security Income. Some marry, or depend on child support payments, or draw on more informal supports. For others, the loss of welfare means further descent into destitution. In the next several chapters, we examine why and how these Texas families leave welfare and what their lives are like afterward. We show that investment in families through supportive services pays dividends in improvements in family life. We demonstrate how families with little access to support may leave welfare for a time, but often remain in poverty and are likely to return to TANF.

THREE

The Weak (and Tangled) Safety Net

SARAH, WHOM WE met in Chapter 1, worked as a nurse's assistant and had cycled on and off the Temporary Assistance to Needy Families (TANF) cash welfare program for several years. She worried that she would need to apply for TANF once again, since even a minor emergency might upset her precarious financial situation. Focused on paying rent and maintaining her truck, she lacked either reliable public or job-related benefits for herself and her children. She received some help from her family but was careful not to rely on them too heavily. She used services from agencies such as food banks, a clothing program, and a local clinic to meet her family's needs.

Sarah was thirty-three years old when we met her. She had an associate's degree as a certified nurse's assistant and wanted more education, but with four children, ages five, seven, nine, and twelve, she lacked the time to pursue further education—any time she was not working she spent with her children.

> If I'm not there to make sure they're doing their stuff, then I'm cheating them. I had my chance to do my stuff, and I didn't do it right. I'm cheating them by not making them do theirs right. I don't have the time to go to school.

Her children were all enrolled in school, and, at the time of our interview, a close friend was helping her out by watching them when school was out.

Sarah had worked most of her life but, as she said, "I had a bad year with my job, so I went on TANF." Sarah continued to struggle financially even when she was receiving TANF. She left the welfare rolls after only a few months, when she found a new job. Sarah had been working at this job for three months when we first met her. She enjoyed her new work, providing basic medical care for people with mental retardation, but disliked the rotating shifts and overtime associated with the job. The overtime pay was welcome, but working different shifts and variable hours proved hard to manage for a mother who depended on friends for child care assistance.

Sarah believed she had to be at her job for three months before her children would be able to requalify for Medicaid. (Her explanation of her family's Medicaid eligibility was confusing to both her and us.) She had received one installment of emergency food stamps before being told she was ineligible for further food stamps. She had also been informed that she owed money to the TANF system because of a data entry error. The pay stub Sarah had submitted to her caseworker on beginning her job was not typed into the agency computer, and as a consequence, during her first month of employment she received a larger TANF payment than she was actually eligible for. Sarah was expecting to receive job-related employee benefits in another month, but her understanding of these benefits was sketchy. She was pretty sure that the employee contribution for benefits was $80 per month, but she was not sure whether her employer had a family health insurance plan.

To support her family, Sarah supplemented her own income with assistance from friends, family members, and local agencies, and by pawning some of her household belongings, including most of her electrical appliances. For example, an aunt bought school clothes and supplies for some of the children. Family members were available to take the children into their homes in case of an emergency. Sarah also received formal support from private social service organizations. In the previous six months, she had been to two different food banks and had received children's school clothes from a local agency. Since no one in the household was on Medicaid, Sarah also struggled to get her children the health care they needed. The free clinic she had been using had begun requiring a $5 co-payment for every visit.

When we met her, Sarah's goals were to get to the point where she could pay rent for an apartment and keep her truck running. She estimated the rent for an apartment to be about $500 per month. Her truck costs, including insurance and upkeep, totaled almost $100 per month. These two expenses together were more than half of her net monthly income. To cope with these two costs, she had to strictly budget all her other expenses. Her children's extracurricular activities had additional costs, such as equipment fees and sports club dues, and during the early fall when we met her she wasn't sure how she was going to pay for these activities. In addition, she lacked the time to become actively involved in her children's activities as either a parent-participant or a volunteer. She also worried that an emergency, or even a brief spell of unemployment, would result in eviction or the loss of her truck. Sarah's economic security was contingent on her keeping her job. In turn, her job depended on many things that were largely outside of her control, including her employer's stability, her own good health and stamina, and the continued health and willingness of the friends and relatives on whom she relied.

The TANF leavers in our study had participated in a major government cash welfare program. Even after exiting the TANF program, most still needed considerable assistance, particularly for medical insurance, child care, and housing. When families had other resources in the form of helpful family members or aid from private social service organizations, and as long as no one in the family had major health problems or other needs, the mother might keep her job, once she found it, for at least a while without further cash assistance from the federal government. Even under these favorable circumstances, however, families almost universally required some additional services—most notably Medicaid, food stamps, public housing assistance, or a child care subsidy. Overall, a large minority of the families we interviewed had to return to TANF at some point.

Thus, while on TANF and in the period immediately after leaving TANF, low-income families drew on a number of additional supports besides their earnings. Some programs, such as the Food Stamp Employment and Training (FSE&T) program and Texas Choices, the state's employment training program for welfare recipients, were designed to assist TANF and food stamp recipients in finding and keeping a job. Others, such as subsidized child care, Medicaid, and food stamp programs, supported necessary expenditures that recent TANF leavers could not afford even when they were employed. This chapter tells the story of how well these statewide government-funded services worked for families leaving welfare. Although it is a convoluted story at times (like the welfare system itself), the data support three key points:

1. Some services are insufficiently funded, so that only a fraction of those eligible can receive them.

2. Many families are ineligible for government services even when they are clearly unable to afford alternatives.

3. The cash welfare system (along with the noncash services usually associated with welfare) is so complicated and demanding that even eligible
   families may find it difficult to successfully apply for and maintain their
   eligibility for these services.

In this context, families in need often seek out other sources of help. They
locate local community organizations and turn to relatives, friends, and neighbors. In this chapter, however, we concentrate on the ways in which the state and
federal systems both assist and fail the low-income families they are designed to
serve.

How the Safety Net Is Supposed to Work

In the post–welfare reform world described in Chapter 1, all families are expected to receive cash welfare benefits for a limited time only. Adult caretakers
(usually parents with dependent children) receiving welfare benefits on behalf
of their children are also required to meet a number of obligations. In particular,
the families we talked with were required to work toward getting a job so that
they could financially support their children without governmental assistance.
If families failed to meet the conditions for welfare receipt, their benefits were
interrupted until they complied with all program requirements. To qualify for
TANF, families had to meet both income and asset eligibility criteria.

TANF recipients also had to sign personal responsibility agreements to en-
gage in specific "responsible behaviors," from detailing their job searches to co-
operating with child support enforcement against the fathers of their children.
They were required to document their children's school attendance and inocula-
tions on an ongoing basis. If successful in qualifying for benefits and maintaining their eligibility, they received a cash grant, which during the study period
was capped at $208 per month for a household of three, the typical size of a
TANF household. In addition, adult TANF recipients were subject to both state
and federal time limits on the receipt of benefits. During the study period, very
few families had reached either set of time limits. (Families who left TANF because they reached time limits were excluded from our study.) Families on TANF
also had access, within constraints, to other programs.

Choices. Unless they had received an exemption based on one of several
special conditions, all adult TANF recipients had to register with and participate
in Choices, the state's job search and employment training program for welfare
users. Entering the Choices program also started the clock ticking for Texas time
limits (which were shorter than the federal five-year lifetime limits, but allowed
TANF caretakers to return to TANF a second time five years after reaching the

state limit). Most Choices activities were focused on helping TANF recipients look for immediate employment. Even the short-term training activities available were quite limited in scope, such as the use of job search facilities. Critics have commented that this program was oriented to place someone in any job, with little regard for income level, benefits, or the stability of the position.

Child Care Subsidies. Because most adults who received TANF were the parents of young children, the state defrayed the cost of child care for Choices families while they prepared for employment and looked for a job. Former TANF families were also eligible to receive child care subsidies for at least a year after leaving TANF with a job, as long as they continued working. Although other low-income families were eligible for subsidized child care, waiting lists for those families were often very long, so that families might never reach the head of the list to receive a child care subsidy.

Medicaid. Both adults and children were eligible for Medicaid health insurance while they were on TANF. However, the picture became more complicated after families left welfare, and eligibility rules differed for adults and children. Adults not on TANF typically could only receive Medicaid:

- For twelve to eighteen months after leaving TANF if they were employed or were forced from TANF due to time limits (known as transitional Medicaid);
- If medical expenses reduced their income below the allowed limit (approximately 24 percent of the poverty level—an almost unachievably low threshold); or
- If they were pregnant and had a family income of less than 185 percent of the poverty level.

The eligibility requirements for Medicaid coverage were less restrictive for children than for adults. Children whose families met asset limitations (they could not own a car worth more than a specified amount or have a savings account) could continue to receive Medicaid if their families earned less than between 100 and 185 percent of the federal poverty line (depending on the age of the child). Given the income levels of the families in this study, almost all children in these families met the income guidelines for Medicaid even when their families were not receiving TANF,[1] even though, for various reasons, not all children had medical coverage. However, the adult program was much more limited, included several tracks, and was controlled by a complicated set of regulations. In many cases, neither the researchers nor the families themselves clearly understood the Medicaid eligibility rules for adults.

Food Stamps. Low-income families were typically eligible to receive food stamps if their households earned less than 130 percent of the federal poverty level and they met other asset and income provisions. Almost all the families in our study should have also been financially eligible for food stamps, regardless of their TANF status. Some non-TANF adults were also required to participate in the FSE&T program in order to receive food stamps. They were required to work thirty hours per week, participate in work-related activities twenty hours per week, or enroll in an education or training program for sixteen to twenty hours per week. Adults were exempt from these requirements if they were caring for children less than six years old, were disabled, were caring for someone who was disabled, or lived in one of the 164 rural counties in Texas that did not operate an FSE&T program.[2]

TANF, Welfare, and Associated Programs: The Experience

In reality, many TANF recipients' experiences did not unfold as envisioned by the state's program planners. Families reported a number of difficulties with the TANF program in terms of accessing the benefit system, understanding the eligibility criteria, and meeting requirements, particularly once they were working. A large number of families never participated in Choices or subsidized child care while receiving TANF assistance. In addition, many families left the program not because they were gainfully employed but because of other circumstances in their lives. Chapter 6 discusses the different reasons behind families' departure from TANF and how these influenced the likelihood that they would receive TANF in the future. Only some families who left TANF actually participated in noncash safety net programs. Those who were able to take advantage of these programs valued their services, but also experienced the programs as erratic and undependable.

TANF recipients often recognized and agreed with the purposes underlying welfare reform. For instance, although visits to the welfare office could be difficult, many clients also thought it reasonable for staff to screen them for eligibility, work readiness, and other factors.

I guess I could see a lot of questions they ask may make some people feel like that [bad]. But if you don't have anything to hide, then what's the difference, you know? The only reason you would feel like that is if you were trying to hide something—you know, that's the way I see it. If you're telling the truth, then there's nothing they can do, you know. And they do check up on everything and maybe that's why because they ask so many questions— but they have to, you know. That's just part of it.

TANF recipients valued both the cash assistance and the supportive services they received when on welfare. For those just beginning or returning to work, even limited TANF assistance helped support their families. Food stamps were distinguished as a particularly valued program by many TANF leavers. As one participant said, "The best thing about having any type of assistance is that my kids always had food. I never had to worry about that."

In general, families recognized the importance of a number of services that they associated with welfare, even though those services were distinct from TANF:

> They have a lot of good programs out, a lot of them I've heard of because of my friends who I baby sit for. Some mothers, you know, they go through all these different programs. They have WIC and you know all that kind of stuff. . . . We went to a clinic, free clinic, independent clinic, that's where I went and got my checkup after I had her, and I think all that stuff is great, you know.

On the other hand, families also described the associated rules and bureaucracy of these programs as complex, error-prone, unforgiving, and degrading to them as individuals. They reported that caseworkers requested the same documentation multiple times, kept clients waiting a long time during scheduled appointments, and discouraged them from applying for services. Although many clients reported working with welfare staff who were polite and respectful, nearly half of the respondents we talked with reported having difficult interactions with the staff. In particular, clients believed that welfare workers negatively stereotyped them.

> Not everybody that comes through the welfare doors, it's not like everybody has never worked. We have had jobs. Situations have just happened or whatever circumstances. And it's like when you go in there, all of the workers are like robots. They are programmed to look down on you.

The long waits reported by respondents were especially problematic for respondents who had carefully planned work and family responsibilities around a scheduled appointment time. Families frequently reported waiting two hours or more in order to see their caseworkers when they had appointments. Respondents who went to the office without an appointment reported all-day waits. Not only could an appointment at the welfare office mean fewer hours worked and paid for, but employers were not always sympathetic to requests for time off from new employees, even for a mandatory appointment. As one respondent noted,

The hardest thing about it is the amount of time that you have to take off [work] in order to get in. And I mean even if you have an appointment, it still takes about five hours.

Another said,

If you're working and you've got to take that time off, it's a real strain on your job. . . . If you're on a job less than ninety days, then you're not supposed to miss any days.

Some clients felt that caseworkers treated welfare recipients either more positively or negatively based on an individual recipient's appearance, behavior, and educational level.

I am educated. And they have always treated me well. I've noticed that what they perceive from you is how they are going to treat you. If I come in, and I'm smacking gum and slapping my kids, telling them to shut up and sit down, and I have rollers in my head and my whole attitude is messed up, then they're going to have an attitude with you. What they [caseworkers] are saying to themselves is, "Oh, god, here comes another one—another person who just doesn't want to work." Well, everybody is not like that. . . . People are judged, they get labeled by their appearance a lot. And it makes a big difference.

In the waiting room, most people are dressed poorly, and you can question what they are doing with their lives. And that is reflected back through the caseworkers.

Some respondents who felt penalized by caseworkers endured what they perceived as unfair treatment as a necessary sacrifice they made for their children. These mothers saw themselves as having little choice but to accept such treatment because they needed the help. As one respondent explained,

I don't care about [the rude treatment]. What else am I going to do? It's for my children. What I don't understand is why these people [caseworkers], if they were giving me money from their own pocket, then that's fine—tell me what you want. But if it is money that is not from your pocket, why do you have to insult and [be] manipulative? It is not your money; you are just working there.

Perhaps the often uneasy relationship between TANF recipients and their caseworkers contributed to the lack of clarity that many recipients had about

TANF eligibility and time limits. One respondent believed that any income at all disqualified her for benefits:

> The only thing with TANF is that you have to be really without any income. You have to have zero income in order to qualify, and at the time I was—I had—I was having some kind of income coming in. They said, "You don't qualify because you have an income."

Another respondent was discouraged from using TANF because she was told that using TANF benefits now would affect her young daughter's future eligibility for TANF as an adult. Many respondents were confused by a rule that linked food stamp eligibility with at least twenty hours per week of paid work.[3] Other respondents found themselves in a double-bind when it came to transportation. Because asset restrictions limited recipients to owning a car of less than $2,000 to $5,000 in value (depending on the program), recipients with reliable cars risked being considered ineligible for benefits. Ironically, recipients very often needed a car to get to the job training they were required to take. In one case, a respondent was allotted $10 a week for transportation expenses to attend a job training program that required a daily ninety-mile round-trip to an area with no public transportation. She explained that no one would be willing to drive her ninety miles each weekday for $10 per week.

Many respondents were still paying back the welfare and food stamp programs for benefits that had been issued them in error. Sometimes these overpayments were not discovered for months. One respondent's welfare benefit was reduced when the welfare office discovered that she had been overpaid three years earlier.

Although many recipients noted that the amount of assistance (TANF and food stamps) varied from month to month, few, if any, were able to explain why their benefit amounts fluctuated. For example, one respondent reported that her TANF check had $70 withheld every month (typically financial penalties for not meeting some requirements of the personal responsibility agreement signed by TANF recipients), but she did not know why this money was being withheld. Another respondent explained that while her TANF benefits had decreased for reasons she did not understand, her food stamps were unpredictable—sometimes larger, sometimes smaller.

> TANF, it went down. And on the food stamps, it just goes, like, it goes a little bit higher, sometimes a little bit lower. It just depends on, I don't know, I guess the worker, or whenever I go back, or what they do give me. . . . Sometimes it's a little bit more, sometimes a little bit less.

Veronica, like other respondents, was in an altercation with the welfare system. She was angry about the back payments of $50 a month charged her by TANF for errors made by the welfare office.

> You know, if I'm sitting here giving you my paychecks and you're entering what you want and not putting the decimal right, that's your mistake. You should fix that. I mean, don't come looking for me, threatening me with laws, talking about welfare fraud. I didn't fraud the welfare, the government. I gave you everything that you asked me for. You tell me to bring you six check stubs; I bring you eight. You are sitting there and you are carrying the numbers onto the computer. You can't run off and tell me my income was miscalculated. Well, I didn't miscalculate it. You know? So how are you going to tell me that I have to pay the government back. . . . I mean, it seems like they're constantly holding you like they want to have something to hold over you. Once I got off welfare, that wasn't good enough. So they . . . send me letters not a month later, not two months, but maybe six or seven months later saying that my income for, this is August now, they sent me a letter saying that I owe them from last year in July.

Another respondent also described a bill she received from TANF for an overpayment from a previous year. She said,

> Last year I was receiving TANF. It was around March of last year. And my boyfriend was working . . . even though we reported that he was working, how much he was making an hour and how many hours he was working a week. You know, his employer filled out that letter. They send you a letter of employment verification when you start any new job, or when you even get fired from a job you have to take this letter to your past employer, no matter how distant it was and have them fill out a letter saying you no longer work there. And we did everything we had to do. And months later, it wasn't soon, it was months later, like about six months later, they sent me a letter saying they had over-issued me a hundred and forty-three dollars in TANF benefits and that I had to repay them. So, I started repaying them. I fought it for a while. I said, "Why do I have to pay these benefits back if you over-issued them to me and I did everything I was supposed to do? You know, I complied with all the rules. I reported that he worked. He filled out that letter from his employer." I go, "And I told you when he stopped working." I said, "And you over-issued me. I didn't over-issue myself."

Still another respondent reported repaying benefits her aunt had received on her behalf when she was still a minor.

When I was younger, I was living with one of my aunts because she lived near the high school that I wanted to attend. So I had to move in with her. And during the four years I lived with her, she was temporarily unemployed. So she applied for food stamp benefits. And she received an over-issuance when I was in her household. So, they started deducting it from me, even though I was a minor child at the time. And it's called recouping . . . so they recouped from my benefits, and they lowered them.

Because TANF's cash value was so low, many families found its greatest usefulness as a gateway to other services rather than as a source of income. In some cases, clients learned about additional available services through the TANF application process.

No, actually that's the reason, that['s] why I went to school, because after I applied for it they sent me a form, like a flier. It was about a program that they had at a community college for women receiving TANF, that if they wanted to go take the classes they could go free of charge. It was because we were receiving TANF and food stamps. So I went and got information, and then I started going to the classes. The only thing that I had to do was receive my GED, which I did before I went to the classes.

Participation in Choices

During the period in which the study took place, 40 percent of TANF adults met the criteria for required participation in Choices. Families could be excused from participation for a number of reasons, including having primary responsibility for a young child (under four years old at the beginning of the study, under two by the end of the period), having a work-impairing physical or mental disability, providing primary care for someone with a disability, or living in a geographically remote area that did not offer employment services.

Significantly more families in the second cohort (the later group of families we tracked), 25 percent, participated in the Choices program in the months prior to leaving TANF than did families in the first cohort, 15 percent (Figure 3.1). The increases in families' participation can be largely explained by a rule change that ended the Choices exemption for mothers of children between the ages of two and four years. Increases in Choices participation occurred before TANF exit, since it assisted in the job hunt that preceded employment and subsequent TANF exit for a number of families.

The qualitative interviews provided even deeper insight into the nature of people's attitudes toward work and the role of Choices in preparing them for

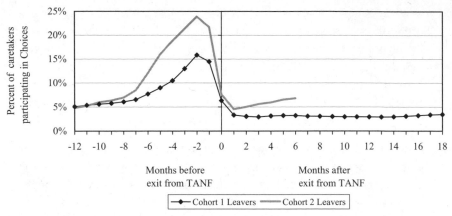

FIGURE 3.1. Caretaker participation in Choices over time. Source: Administrative data from the Texas Department of Human Services and the Texas Workforce Commission for cases leaving TANF from April 1998 through June 1999 (Cohort 1) or from July through September 2000 (Cohort 2).

employment. Welfare recipients usually were eager to work and valued services and supports they perceived as helpful to them in entering the labor force.

> I think you are better off working because you can depend on yourself, your kids are proud of you, and you can buy what you need.

In particular, they appreciated case management activities that facilitated intensive and long-term training and job search assistance. Respondents tended to complain about the absence of job training and placement activities rather than about being forced to participate in them. In fact, most respondents responded enthusiastically to the programs that were available. When computers were available, respondents used them to access job notices on-line: "I used to go—I used to get on the computers and look for jobs. They have that computer stuff there [Choices office]."

When respondents received case management to help them take advantage of programs and resources, they often spoke highly of the services that they received.

> I went through a week of class, and they encouraged me. They do a lot of encouraging. And the ladies are real friendly. They like to have fun with what they do. And they encourage you to get your GED, to go to college. I mean, they just fill your head up. And it is things you can do if you just put mind to it. It's all about what you want to do. And they sat me down and talked

to me because I think that I was the youngest one in there. All the other women were older than me. And they talked to me, and they were asking me what I wanted to do. And they kept telling me that I was intelligent and all this, and it got to my head. So, I went out and I applied for me a job and I got it.

In some cases, clients participated in long-term, multisupport programs, though usually through avenues other than Choices or in addition to Choices. These programs often coordinated supports such as child care, housing, and transportation, in addition to providing more extensive training and education than was available through Choices. Respondents spoke glowingly about them.

And the training program that I was in, it helped me to go through anger management and self-control. I was very angry. And how to get along with your co-workers and family. I learned a lot out of the program. My counselor that I had when I was going there, she helped me a lot. I enjoyed the training program. I was in there for eleven months, and then I got placed in job placement. I went on job search and everything to look for work, and I finally got hired in January.

Respondents sometimes credited a supportive caseworker, in Choices or in other programs, for contributing to their motivation and success on the job market.

I've been in the Choices program and I have a caseworker at the Workforce [local workforce center]. I'm in the Choices program, and she's wonderful. She helps me out a lot. She tells me things and she just helps me out a lot. She gives me ideas and she does what she can to help me because she understands the situation.

In summary, respondents appreciated the way that TANF facilitated access to other even more valued programs, such as Choices, Medicaid, and child care subsidies. Though useful, the cash benefit was relatively small and unreliable. In addition, required visits to welfare offices were inconvenient and sometimes were themselves a barrier to employment when they interfered with time spent on the job.

Most of our respondents agreed in principle with the welfare system's work requirements. They believed that they should support themselves through work and wanted to have jobs. They felt discouraged when they could not find jobs or were unable to make the accommodations necessary to sustain employment, such as arranging for child care or transportation. Respondents were particularly enthusiastic about the educational opportunities they were able to access through TANF. They highly valued services that supported their work effort. One respondent commented,

> One advantage is that they [caseworkers] help you when you don't have a job or the necessary resources. They also help you find a job, and that's a big advantage.

Overall, in discussing their experience with the welfare system and TANF offices, welfare leavers made distinctions between difficulties that were associated with individual caseworkers and broader issues associated with TANF policies. Respondents expressed a range of attitudes and responses about their experiences in the welfare system. Many women experienced the TANF application process, which asked direct and highly personal questions (sometimes in settings with little privacy), as intimidating and intrusive. However, some of the same women also supported welfare policies that encouraged employment, and thus accepted the strict eligibility requirements and the need to recertify for benefits periodically.

Subsidized Child Care

Among employed families with young children who left TANF—the population most likely to need subsidized child care—administrative data indicate that less than a third (between 22 and 30 percent, depending on the cohort) actually received child care subsidies at the time they left TANF (Figure 3.2). Although employed families should have been eligible for transitional child care subsidies for at least twelve months after leaving TANF, the percentage of families in subsidized child care slowly declined over time.

According to survey responses, almost all financial assistance for child care was obtained through the state's Child Care Management System (CCMS), a subsidy system (Table 3.1). Only a small fraction of the families we interviewed used formal child care arrangements, and an even smaller fraction received support from the CCMS. Thus, most child care occurred through informal arrangements with family or friends as caregivers. The statewide survey showed that less than 20 percent of employed TANF leavers left their children in the care of nonrelatives. In addition, a small minority of families, just under 10 percent, relied on older children (those older than nine or ten years) to care for themselves. Generally, respondents' children were left in the care of their parents or close relatives.

Although some mothers may have preferred the child care provided by extended family members, often reliance on them was the result of a family's in-

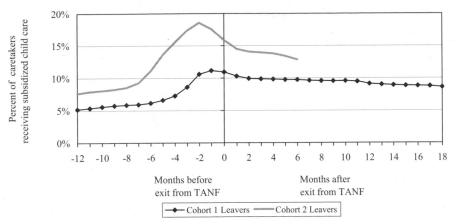

FIGURE 3.2.   Subsidized child care receipt by employed parents of young children before and after leaving TANF. Source: Administrative data from the Texas Department of Human Services for cases leaving TANF from April 1998 through June 1999 (Cohort 1) or from July through September 2000 (Cohort 2).

ability to obtain a child care subsidy. Families who applied for child care subsidies seemed unclear about the program requirements and were often placed on long waiting lists for services. In contrast, mothers who actually received child care subsidies, often because they had been prioritized on the waiting list, talked favorably about the program's ability to meet their child care needs:

> I have school and need to take care of my son. He is diagnosed with ADHD and needs to take medication every three hours. The day care he attends has the medication, too, as well as my mom when she takes him. My son attends a special program at the elementary school. At night when I'm at school, my mom watches him. He also requires medication for sleeping. I talked to one of my friends whose child is in the Head Start program, and she told me to look into the special program. He qualified for the program because he has a disability (ADHD) and they tested him. Also, because I was on welfare, I immediately qualified.

Although families highly valued the services that child care subsidy programs provided, actually getting and maintaining child care subsidies was quite difficult. Child care subsidy regulations created double-binds for respondents. While Choices participants were supposed to receive child care for job search activities, others did not receive subsidized child care until they were employed or in an appropriate training program, and might not have priority even then. At the same time, they were limited in their ability to search for jobs or the best

**Table 3.1. Financial Assistance with Child Care
(of All Families Leaving TANF), Cohort 2**

Total number of survey respondents: 723

Type of financial assistance with child care received	Share of total respondents
CCMS (state child care subsidies)	14.7%
Church	0.6%
Community group	1.5%
Other	0.8%

Source: Statewide survey of families leaving TANF in July–
September 2000.

educational programs when they had no one to care for their children while they were engaged in these activities.

> But the classes—you know, I thought that once your exemption came in that you could choose to go. Or like I had been exempt when I found a job, and you know they said they'll give me child care and I was going to get it for her, but I had to work twenty hours first in order to get the child care, and I was like, well, I'm not going to get the twenty hours first. I've got to have child care in order to go.

Families also struggled to keep the child care subsidies they had obtained. For example, subsidies could be revoked if children were absent from child care for too many days, even when they were absent because of illness. Thus, as one mother explained, it was possible to lose your child care at a time when your job was in the greatest jeopardy. After staying home from work to care for her ill child, this mother lost both her child care subsidy, because of her child's absence from care, and her job, when her work absences extended beyond the child's illness due to her loss of child care.

Medicaid and Health Insurance

When on TANF, an entire family was eligible for Medicaid, and usually enrolled in the program. The increase in families on Medicaid prior to TANF exit reflects family entry into TANF during the months preceding exit. Some families were on TANF for relatively short spells before exit. Once families left TANF, however,

Medicaid eligibility became a much more confusing and variable proposition. So, while almost all family members received Medicaid shortly before leaving TANF, the number of families with Medicaid dropped precipitously when families left welfare. In fact, only 20 percent of adults and children received Medicaid without interruption once their TANF cases were closed. Although one-half of families regained Medicaid for at least some of their children, many families spent the post-TANF period without any form of health insurance.

In the several months following exit from TANF, Medicaid receipt increased to around 40 percent for adults in the administrative database (Figure 3.3) and 60 percent for children (Figure 3.4), and remained near those levels for most of the year after TANF exit. Increases in adults' Medicaid receipt over time were likely due to former recipients returning to TANF. Children's Medicaid receipt after leaving TANF was less affected than adults', since many children were eligible for some Medicaid programs. The dip in Medicaid receipt twelve months after departure from TANF most likely reflects the expiration of transitional Medicaid benefits for employed caretakers. After the first quarter following exit, increases and decreases in Medicaid receipt for children mirrored the patterns of decline observed for their parents.

We learned in the qualitative interviews that some former TANF recipients believed that their Medicaid coverage was linked to TANF and assumed that they, and to a lesser extent their children, were no longer eligible for Medicaid after leaving TANF. In fact, Medicaid was not automatically continuous when

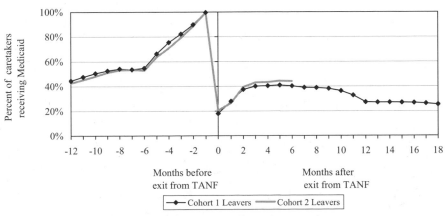

FIGURE 3.3. Adult Medicaid receipt before and after leaving TANF. Source: Administrative data from the Texas Department of Human Services for cases leaving TANF from April 1998 through June 1999 (Cohort 1) or from July through September 2000 (Cohort 2).

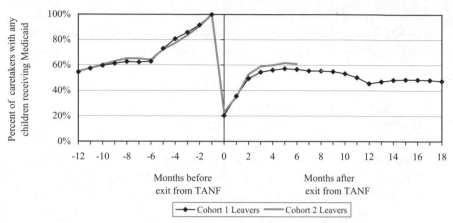

FIGURE 3.4.   Children's Medicaid receipt before and after leaving TANF. Source: Administrative data from the Texas Department of Human Services for cases leaving TANF from April 1998 through June 1999 (Cohort 1) or from July through September 2000 (Cohort 2).

TANF ended; the Medicaid system required that families report their employ- ment within a specified time after leaving TANF in order to receive transitional Medicaid.

Similar to the TANF application process, parents applying for Medicaid for themselves and their children were expected to produce required documenta- tion and attend scheduled certification appointments. Some parents were unable to fulfill these requirements without putting their jobs at risk. Confusion about application and recertification requirements and barriers to meeting them con- tributed to the drop in respondents' Medicaid use over time.

> *Respondent:* I thought since TANF ended, then that's why Medicaid ended. And I couldn't get medical benefits from my job yet, because I had to be there six months and I hadn't been.
> *Interviewer:* Did you ever get Medicaid again, for you or your kids?
> *Respondent:* No, no.

And another respondent:

> I had all of them [Medicaid, food stamps, TANF] but when they cut me off of TANF they cut me [and my children] off Medicaid.

Respondents who reapplied for benefits often experienced confusion about the programs for which they had actually applied. Applications for TANF, Medic- aid, and food stamps seemed interchangeable, and some applicants discovered what services they had actually filed for only after the fact. Our interviews often reflected their confusion.

> We had Medicaid since the last time I applied for food stamps. I only had the Medicaid, but then I reapplied again but [apparently] not for Medicaid. Recently they told me that my Medicaid had run out and I needed to reapply. No one has Medicaid right now, and I'm not receiving food stamps either.

Many respondents did not understand that they or, even more likely, their children were still possibly eligible for Medicaid after leaving TANF. A smaller number understood they were potentially eligible but were confused about the application system. Many TANF leavers commented on the problems they faced without health insurance when their Medicaid participation ended.

In at least one case among our respondents, the absence of Medicaid coverage had dire results for the family. Soon after realizing she was pregnant, one mother we spoke with applied for Medicaid.

> It wasn't until I was seven months' pregnant that I went to ask for Medicaid. I had to ask for emergency [assistance]. I told someone there that I really needed Medicaid because I am up in age and I don't know how my baby is doing. I was really scared that something would happen to him. I had a lot of problems with the pregnancy because I couldn't go to the doctor since I had no money. I went to apply for Medicaid and the lady did not give me Medicaid. Many times I put in an application and went to interviews.

However, for reasons that she never understood, her emergency case was not accepted. She only knew that she never seemed successful in meeting all the application demands.

> She did not explain to me. She just kept asking me for papers. Every time I went she would ask me for something else. Every time.

A prenatal checkup at a free clinic revealed that her baby was experiencing heart problems. Instead of receiving immediate medical attention, the mother was scheduled for a follow-up appointment during the next week to review her Medicaid application. The baby died in utero the day before this scheduled appointment.

> If they knew that my baby had problems, they should have done something at that time. They should have taken me to the doctor immediately, but since I still didn't have Medicaid. . . .

Although it is impossible to know whether the baby would have survived with proper prenatal care, the baby's death seemed to the mother to be related to the family's lack of means and their lack of access to health care. The respondent's husband, whose physical disabilities limited his ability to work, was unemployed at the time of the baby's death.

> My husband was not working. We were asking around for money. My husband went out on the streets to ask for money for the funeral.

The family was also without electricity during a portion of the hot and humid summer months after their utilities were turned off. Agencies that assisted families with rent and utility payments often restricted their grants to only once a year per family. A family like this one who had received assistance during the past twelve months was no longer eligible for the program. Not surprisingly, food had also been in short supply at the time of the baby's death. When asked if the family had ever suffered from lack of food, the respondent replied,

> Yes, last year when my baby died we did not have anything—nothing to eat. It was terrible.

Food Stamps

By our own estimation, most families in our study were financially eligible for food stamps even after they left TANF. However, families' participation in the food stamps program, which steadily increased after they went on TANF, fell off sharply after they left TANF. Three-fourths of these families received food stamps two months prior to TANF exit—a figure that dropped to 37 percent at TANF exit and continued to decline to 30 percent by the end of the eighteen-month follow-up period (Figure 3.5).

Respondents had less frequent misunderstandings about and difficulties with the food stamp program. However, the food stamp program was not trouble-free. In particular, the welfare leavers we spoke with described challenges associated with the food stamp application process after departure from TANF and with the eligibility criteria for the FSE&T program. Some respondents believed the same criteria were used to determine both TANF and food stamp eligibility.

> I was pretty sure that if we did not qualify for TANF, that we wouldn't qualify for food stamps.

Still other respondents did not understand how the food stamps application process differed from their TANF application.

> I never got an application for food stamps, and I didn't know that April was the last month. [We—the research group—were unsure what program restrictions this respondent was referring to.]

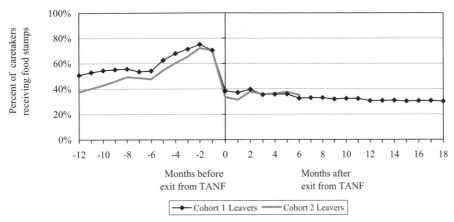

FIGURE 3.5. Use of food stamps before and after leaving TANF. Source: Administrative data from the Texas Department of Human Services for cases leaving TANF from April 1998 through June 1999 (Cohort 1) or from July through September 2000 (Cohort 2).

Respondents described receiving information about food stamps in many different ways: from staff at the Texas Department of Human Services and the Texas Workforce Commission offices, from the offices of other agencies they visited, and from other community members—neighbors, friends and relatives. Although respondents usually identified and trusted the information they heard about food stamp benefits, they often appeared to misunderstand the program.

The stringent and confusing eligibility requirements and the links (or assumed links) among programs made it difficult for families to make use of the safety net of benefits to which they might well have been entitled. In many cases, families coped with problems and emergencies on their own, without the services that might have improved their families' health and well-being. In turn, program bureaucracies at times had a negative effect both on family functioning and on achieving success at a new job.

Overall, families leaving TANF faced a complex and fractured set of transitional and maintenance services. They often misunderstood program eligibility guidelines and did not have the resources to meet application demands. Under these conditions, mothers who struggled to support their families while working in low-wage jobs often did so without health insurance benefits, child care assistance, or, less frequently, food stamps.[4] In the next chapter we examine in even greater detail this struggle to make ends meet, by exploring families' sources of household income.

FOUR

Making a Living After Welfare

Where Does the Money Come From?

WHEN WE MET her, Ann was a twenty-two-year-old mother whose TANF benefits had ended about six months previously. Dealing simultaneously with many
issues, Ann longed for financial stability, as well as stability in other important
areas of her life. She had only limited education, having dropped out of school
after the eighth grade and still lacking a GED. She had two children, but, although she had recently married (and since separated), her husband was not
the father of the children. Ann had applied for government assistance for the
first time when she was a teenager alone and pregnant—her children's father
was incarcerated. "I was struggling. I didn't have any financial help, and I wasn't
working."

At that time, Ann received Temporary Assistance for Needy Families (TANF),
as well food stamps and Medicaid for herself and her children. Later, during
another difficult time in her life, when she left her children's father, she turned
again to TANF for financial assistance. When we met Ann, she and her second
husband had recently separated and no longer shared a household. Although
the separation had created financial pressures for her, Ann was not receiving any
type of government assistance. She and her two children had moved into her
sister's home two months before our interview. Two adults and three children

shared the subsidized apartment. The lease was in Ann's sister's name, and Ann did not pay any rent or contribute to utilities. Ann also had access to her sister's telephone without charge.

For the previous six months, Ann had been working forty hours per week as an assembly-line worker earning $6.40 per hour. This job also provided her (but not her children) with limited medical and dental insurance. She owned a car, which she drove daily to and from work, but she could not afford the renewal on her automobile insurance, a requirement in Texas.

Her fixed monthly costs included a $266 car payment, $80 for gasoline, $50 for a storage unit that held all of her belongings, and $50 for groceries. She and her sister shared care for their children. In the month before our interview, she had spent almost $400 on needed car repairs. Because Ann was not officially on the lease of her sister's apartment, she did not have an address to use for food stamps or Medicaid applications. She and her sister lived in fear of losing their housing, since all of them could be evicted if the housing authority learned that Ann and her children were sharing the apartment.

Like many of those we interviewed, Ann had neither a checking account nor a savings account. Also, like many respondents, she took advantage of pawn shops, having used them in the past as a source of immediate emergency income. After paying her monthly bills, Ann reported having about $15 left at the end of the month. Ann might experience this small monthly surplus only when there were no unanticipated expenses. However, this had never happened that she could remember, since each month that passed seemed to bring with it a new financial crisis.

Ann's employment history consisted of a number of short-term positions at temporary jobs. At her current low-wage job, even without having to pay rent and utilities, Ann barely managed to meet her monthly financial obligations. Any number of events—repossession of a car, loss of her job, illness, a disagreement with her sister, or an eviction—would have irreparably upset the careful balance of resources that Ann had crafted to support her family.

Ann's case illustrates some of the complex factors affecting welfare leavers. With little opportunity to increase her earnings and no current access to social services, she was barely surviving in a steady, low-wage job. Indeed, compared with other respondents, Ann might have been considered unusual—even fortunate—to have located a manufacturing job that came with some benefits, including individual health insurance, paid vacation, and sick leave.

Even with steady full-time work, Ann was able to provide for her family only because of the housing her sister in turn provided her. With her current salary and monthly expenses, she would have been unable to pay rent or utilities on her own. Thus, Ann's family was only as stable as her sister's housing and Ann's current job were. And Ann had been at her current job for only a relatively short time.

Welfare Reform and Income

Although this chapter is concerned with employment and the nature of the jobs welfare recipients found as they left welfare, welfare recipients also left welfare for reasons unrelated to employment. For example, some respondents left TANF when they got married, qualified for a disability pension, or began to receive child support. Except for those recipients who left because they qualified for Supplemental Security Income (SSI, or disability support), recipients were often still dependent on someone else's income, either directly or indirectly, in order to leave TANF. If their marriage, their child support payments, or their access to pension income ceased, they would immediately face financial challenges.

Those who left TANF within the study period did so at a time when the economy was vigorous and growing. Without available jobs, respondents would have been unable to find employment, their children's fathers would not have earned enough to pay child support, and a new partner could not have contributed as much to the support of the household. The role of the economy is particularly relevant to our study in that the onset of welfare reform occurred during an economic boom. Although economists and policy-makers seem to agree that this economy produced jobs that allowed more people to leave welfare, they disagree about the wages and types of jobs that were produced (Boushey and Rosnick, 2003). The growth economy of the 1990s made it much more possible for those leaving welfare to find work. Still, as Ann's case illustrates, many of these former recipients could not advance either financially or materially on the income from the jobs they found. Many welfare leavers in our study found employment but still generated too little in the way of resources to stabilize their households. In particular, many women we interviewed worked in jobs without regular hours or steady income, and these jobs typically were highly inflexible in their ability to respond to the personal and family needs of the employed mother.

Other researchers have estimated that it costs families with young children between $300 and $400 per month to absorb the additional costs associated with being employed (Edin and Lein, 1997). The associated costs of employment for welfare leavers' families included expenses for transportation to and from a job, increased rents when housing subsidies lapsed, private medical insurance, new job-related clothing, and, often particularly costly, child care. Because the rates in the decentralized child care system in Texas are unaffordable for families at or near poverty, most families must choose between acquiring an elusive child care subsidy or using an informal source of child care. Unfortunately, child care subsidies for low-income families reach only a small fraction of the families that are eligible.

More than half of the families we interviewed left TANF because they found employment. However, a number left for other reasons as well. In this chapter, we examine their success in providing adequate support for their households by whatever means, stabilizing their families, and staying off welfare for extended time periods. We found through our interviews that, with a few exceptions, families who left TANF to marry or because of child support payments felt vulnerable and highly dependent on another person's job stability. If the wage earner lost income or employment, women depending on the husband's earnings or on child support from their children's father often returned to TANF, at least in the short term. (However, as we discuss later, analysis of administrative data indicated that such families were more stable than others in staying off TANF.)

In general, even families with jobs, dependent on SSI, or receiving child support still utilized multiple economic strategies to sustain their households. They combined earned income, child support, and other cash transfers simultaneously. They may have used the Earned Income Tax Credit (EITC) to meet expenses. However, none of these strategies lifted the families we talked with out of poverty, and consequently, families remained vulnerable to a destabilizing event that could result in their return to the TANF rolls. We examine in turn families' experiences with jobs, child support, the EITC, and other sources of income.

Earning One's Way: Jobs After Welfare

Both the administrative data and the survey and ethnographic data from our research project documented families' efforts to gain employment and, once employed, the difficulties they experienced in stabilizing their households. As described in Chapter 2, we found that the parents in welfare-leaving families wanted to work, and about half of them were able to find work. However, very few welfare leavers were able to find a job that provided enough in wages to regularly support family life, and even though many of these families supplemented their incomes with other resources, their average wage hovered just below the poverty level. Most employment remained tenuous, and relatively few welfare leavers remained with the same employer continuously.

Families had several reasons for wanting to work. Parents wanted to be free of the bureaucratic welfare process, move their families out of poverty, and perform as good role models for their children:

I think you are better off working, because you can depend on yourself, your kids are proud of you, and you can buy what you need.

The welfare leavers we heard from believed that employment was good for themselves and their families. In both the survey and the intensive interviews, family members sometimes described themselves as employed even when they had earned no income in the previous month. For example, several respondents were registered with temporary agencies, substitute teacher systems, or other on-call services. Although they described themselves as employed, they had not been placed in any position and had not earned any income recently. Furthermore, respondents who had been laid off from jobs in the preceding several months often described themselves as still employed if they were waiting and hoping to be recalled to their jobs. One respondent commented, "Oh, boy, I still have my job . . . but I haven't worked since August." Another respondent described herself as employed after accepting but before starting a new job.

Although the desire for employment seemed to be a consistent theme across all aspects of this study, it manifested itself differently in the administrative and interview data. In the administrative data, we saw welfare leavers cycle into and out of jobs, returning to TANF between employment spells, but generally returning to the job market. Similarly, about 28 percent of the respondents we talked with directly returned to welfare within short periods of time. However, those returning to TANF were greatly outnumbered by the recipients who were moving off the welfare rolls, many of them heading back to low-wage, low-stability jobs. For a number of reasons, however, parents who worked were unlikely to retain jobs for extended periods of time, and were also unlikely to earn wages much above the poverty level.

The Nature of Work

The administrative data confirmed that employment was indeed the primary source of income for poor families leaving TANF. Approximately 55 percent of TANF leavers were employed when they left TANF, and 70 percent were employed for some time in the year after their departure from TANF (Figure 4.1). A portion of these leavers maintained consistent employment over time, with 33 percent of this group employed in all four calendar quarters after they left TANF.

The earnings of employed TANF leavers increased just before their exit from TANF (Figure 4.2), which likely caused many families to become financially ineligible for continued TANF benefits, contributing to their departure from welfare. On average, employed leavers earned around $2,000 in the calendar quarter

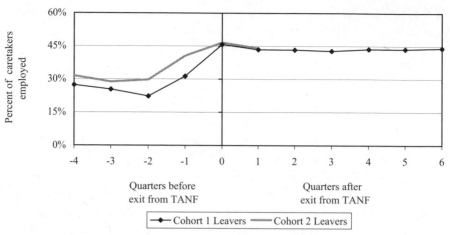

FIGURE 4.1.   Employment of TANF leavers before and after leaving TANF, by quarter.
Source: Administrative data from the Texas Department of Human Services and the
Texas Workforce Commission for cases leaving TANF from April 1998 through June 1999
(Cohort 1) or from July through September 2000 (Cohort 2).

when they left TANF, and their earnings increased in the next eighteen months.
By the end of the study, employed leavers averaged $2,500 in quarterly earnings,
about 75 percent of the poverty level for a family of three. Even for those with
stable employment (employment in all four quarters), quarterly earnings averaged only between $2,500 and $2,800 per quarter, with annual earnings totaling
on average about $10,800, substantially below the poverty line for a household
of three.

The rates of employment captured by the mail survey were in line with the
administrative data. Of the 723 leavers who participated in the statewide mail-
telephone survey (having left TANF during the summer of 2000), 46 percent reported that they were employed at the time of survey completion. Employed respondents reported a median hourly wage of $6.25 per hour (half of the reported
salaries were above this hourly rate and half were below it). Most of the employed respondents were fairly new to their current jobs, having been employed
there for approximately five months, or since shortly after they left TANF. About
six in every ten respondents (60 percent) had conducted a job search within the
past six months, suggesting that even some employed respondents had probably
been unemployed or underemployed at some time since leaving TANF. Furthermore, almost a third of the unemployed respondents reported working in the
past six months. Thus, while some workers were employed in all four quarters
after leaving TANF, others cycled between employment and unemployment.

Reflecting larger trends in the U.S. labor market, respondents most often reported working in the retail and health care industries. Clerical/secretarial jobs were the occupations most frequently cited by survey respondents, followed by cashier positions and cook/waitress/restaurant work. Home health care worker and nursing assistant were also commonly listed occupations. Most of these occupations were located in the service industry sector of the economy and could be characterized as positions that typically offered little stability and few benefits.

The level of benefits available to the welfare leavers in our statewide survey was low. Although respondents valued health benefits particularly for their families as well as for themselves, other job benefits, such as paid sick days, paid vacation time, paid holidays, and personal days, when available, allowed workers to address family matters during the work week without losing wages and still maintain their status as responsible workers. After transitional Medicaid assistance was exhausted, employer-provided health insurance was likely the only avenue to health insurance for a wage-earning, low-income mother for herself and her children.[1] Without access to company-sponsored health insurance, many mothers, even mothers whose children received public health insurance through Medicaid were uninsured and, as a result, often had to forgo medical treatment for temporary or more chronic health conditions.

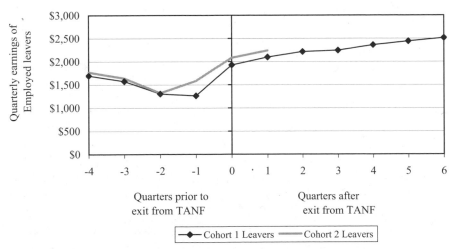

FIGURE 4.2. Quarterly earnings over time for TANF leavers with any earnings. Source: Administrative data from the Texas Department of Human Services and the Texas Workforce Commission for cases leaving TANF from April 1998 through June 1999 (Cohort 1) or from July through September 2000 (Cohort 2).

Table 4.1. Occupation by Educational Attainment, Cohort 2

	All (N = 333)	Grade <9 (N = 32)	Grades 9–12 (N = 191)	Grade >12 (N = 110)
Clerical/secretary/clerk	16.6%	11.5%	7.6%	32.7%
Cashier	12.5%	0%	17.8%	5.6%
Cook/waitress/worker	11.9%	38.5%	13.0%	3.7%
Health care provider	8.8%	0%	11.9%	5.6%
Industrial/manufacturing	8.4%	15.4%	9.2%	5.6%
Sales/retail	7.2%	7.7%	6.5%	8.4%
Housekeeping/custodial	6.9%	11.5%	8.6%	2.8%

Source: Statewide survey of TANF leavers in July–September 2000.
Note: N for each category denotes the total number of employed respondents in that category.

Approximately 29 percent of the employed survey respondents reported receiving some employee benefits, most typically vacation time (21 percent), followed by some form of health insurance benefit (17 percent) or paid sick days (18 percent). An additional 17 percent said that they couldn't afford their contribution or co-payments for the health benefits offered by their employers. However, a majority of wage earners did not receive any of these benefits. Those who did receive job-related benefits, such as health insurance, found their coverage interrupted when their jobs ended.

Not surprisingly, jobs were not randomly distributed among welfare leavers. Respondents with higher levels of education obtained higher-paying jobs, particularly in clerical and secretarial positions. Thirty-three percent of respondents with some college experience reported being employed in clerical or secretarial jobs. Respondents with less than a ninth grade education were heavily concentrated in restaurant and fast food occupations, 39 percent, compared with only 4 percent of those in this job category among those with some college education. The jobs most frequently mentioned are categorized according to the respondents' educational level in Table 4.1.

In addition to low wages and low benefit levels, the working experience was characterized by considerable job instability. Both the survey responses and the administrative data supported this finding. According to the mail-phone survey, 32 percent of the 723 respondents had worked more than one job during the preceding six months. Twenty-five percent of the employed survey respondents reported having a temporary job (see Lambert et al., 2002, for a discussion of job instability). Interview respondents also participated in temporary forms of employment. The respondents we interviewed worked at migratory farm labor, school district dining hall and janitorial work, grocery work, seasonal gardening or plant nursery work, and in the tourist industry. Many of these jobs were by their nature temporary. For example, jobs in construction might last only a few days. Domestic work might end when employers went on vacation or moved. The temporary or seasonal nature of these jobs was reflected in respondents' utilization of the TANF program. Irregular employment often contributed to the sometimes erratic cycling on and off welfare. With the notable exception of school district employment, most irregular employment provided few or no benefits and small, irregular paychecks that made saving for the future difficult, if not impossible. Further, those laid off from such jobs had little security about the prospects of being rehired.

Among those employed, one-quarter (25 percent) reported participating in temporary or seasonal employment. However, a greater proportion of respondents of color reported participating in temporary employment than white respondents. Nearly three out of ten of both Black (29 percent) and Hispanic (28 percent) respondents were employed on a temporary basis, compared with less than a fifth of white respondents (18 percent). Overall, survey respondents typically had been employed for less than a year (not surprising, given that they had all left TANF less than a year earlier), received no work-related benefits, and were paid just a little above minimum wage.

To provide a more textured description of the range of job possibilities available to welfare leavers, we characterized interviewed respondents' employment as falling into five types, based on level of wages and job stability: doing well, stable employment but low pay, underemployment, low-security employment, and very low-income jobs or off-the-books employment. Because urban and rural employment tended to exhibit structural differences, we also describe some of the circumstances surrounding employment in rural areas.

Doing Well. A small minority, fewer than ten of the 179 leavers we interviewed, had completed substantial educational programs and entered professional occupations such as teaching and nursing. Notably, most had completed their training prior to experiencing the life crisis that had precipitated their use of welfare. This relatively small group had jobs with incomes above the poverty line and considerable promise of stability. One respondent began her account of a typical day this way:

I get up and go to school. Now that I'm working, I mean—I work as a teacher so I go to school. . . .

When asked about her pay, she replied,

I think the starting salary for teachers is $29,000 to $30,000. You get more because you're bilingual. In Texas you get a $3,000 raise—so about $33,000. That is not bad for a single mom with one child.

Aside from this relatively small group of less than ten respondents, it was difficult to determine how many workers participated in each of the four remaining patterns, since workers combined patterns or changed among them over time.

Stable Employment But Low Pay. Another larger group of welfare leavers found jobs that were low-paying but relatively stable. It proved difficult to gauge the precise number of respondents who had settled into relatively stable positions, however. While they might earn income regularly, and certainly in each quarter, they still described relatively unstable jobs. Given their status as recent welfare leavers, almost none had been in their current job longer than a year. Though many respondents hoped to be in their jobs for some time, the accounts of many respondents showed that even jobs that promised considerable stability could easily unravel. A respondent described the nature of such job transitions, even in what she hoped was a permanent position:

Respondent: I go in at seven in the morning, and I get off at six, every day. And I only have one day off, which is Sunday. . . .
   Interviewer: How long have you been working with this company?
   Respondent: I started . . . actually, they laid me off. I just got another job with the same company. I was there nine months when they laid me off. But, you know, I'm a hustler. I'm not going to come home and sit and cry because they fired me or they laid me off. So the first thing I did, I went and called my agency again. And I told them the situation. So they offered me another job with the same company. Right now I'm with a temp, but next month they're going to make me full-time.

This respondent described moving from a permanent to a temporary position and anticipated moving again into a permanent position, all while working at the same company. At least part of the time, however, she was actually the contractual employee of a temporary placement agency.

Underemployment. Most respondents wanted to be employed, and some reported being employed even when they had not earned any income in the previous month. This pattern was only one of several underemployment patterns among the welfare leavers we interviewed. Some workers rotated between periods of employment and periods of unemployment. Others were almost always employed, but for fewer hours than they wanted and needed. Some respondents referred to occasional day jobs as employment:

> I have been flopping around on different jobs here lately that's good in pay and also that I enjoy doing, which I just got a new one today. So, hopefully it will work out ... I'm doing housecleaning for ... residential homes and people that move out of homes and they need it cleaned up.

Self-reported employment figures should be considered cautiously, since such occupations may only provide a few hours of work each week. Similarly, even workers with reported earnings in every quarter may be employed relatively few hours each quarter.

Low-Security Employment. Many employed respondents in their first or second (the job they took when the first one didn't work out) jobs were engaged in work that was irregularly scheduled. These respondents often experienced only limited job security.

> I got a temporary full-time position as an aide for a child at a hospital. So it's going to last maybe up to Thanksgiving, maybe Christmas if I'm lucky. [The interview took place in early November.]

Very Low-Income Jobs or Off-the-Books Employment. Respondents we interviewed often received very low wages, sometimes below the minimum wage. Furthermore, they often misrepresented the low level of income they were currently receiving, so the self-reported income figures from our interviews and surveys may be somewhat inflated. For instance, some respondents who were anticipating a future raise reported their current pay at the higher rate, even though they had not yet received their raise. One respondent, when asked about her pay, explained:

> I have an evaluation, so I will be getting a raise. I'll be making about eleven hundred a month.

Other respondents reported relatively high rates of hourly pay but very few hours of work per week. Still others reported very low rates of pay. Such low rates were particularly prevalent among women who worked for other individuals or families as babysitters, housecleaners, or yard workers. They usually were paid off the books. Such jobs were often reimbursed in cash, not reported to the government, and not taxed. Some short-term agricultural work could also be included in this category. Hourly rates and the weekly hours worked varied considerably among such jobs, and in some situations the pay was by the piece, making it difficult to compute an hourly wage. For example, one household reported all adult and teenage members having full-time employment because the family had a contract to hoe ten acres of cotton for $10 per acre, a task that would take them more than a week. Yet another household was employed picking peppers for $2.40 per sack of peppers without stems or $2.00 per sack with stems. The compensation to the family averaged anywhere from $300 to $450 per week during the few weeks of harvest.

Rural Work. Rural settings presented families with distinctive employment problems. In rural Jasper County, for instance, the most prevalent forms of employment available to study participants were minimum-wage service jobs, with discount operations and fast food establishments serving as leading employers. Because jobs were limited, the competition for them was intense. Several rural respondents searched months for a job before obtaining their current minimum-wage positions. Since these jobs, which offered solid employment with at least minimum-wage pay, were few and highly prized, families' social contacts were often the only way to get access to them. Respondents explained that higher-paying jobs were often reserved for those who "had connections" or knew someone at a business or corporation who could "pull strings" to get them hired. For example, one respondent commented that, because she knew someone and had a reputation as a good cook, she was able to get one of the better-paying jobs in Jasper as a chef. According to many Jasper respondents, race and ethnicity played a determining role in who held certain jobs. During our three-week stay in Jasper, respondents pointed out a number of employers, including several fast food establishments, they believed would not hire Black workers. Thus, Black respondents felt even more constrained in their job opportunities in these communities. These differences in access to employment contributed to marked income differences between the Blacks and the whites we interviewed in one rural site (Table 4.2).

When respondents in rural areas had specific occupational skills, they still sometimes had difficulty finding jobs related to their skills. For example, one nurse was first employed by a hospital that later closed. After losing this job, she was unable to find another nursing job in Jasper. Without a car and without public transportation between neighboring cities, commuting to another community for work became impossible. Respondents reported that, not only was there no bus service, but there was only one local cab in Jasper. That single cab only made trips within Jasper and did not offer service to other communities.

In Plainview, a rural city in the Texas Panhandle, jobs followed the agricultural cycle. During the time of our interviews, in late fall, we met a number

Table 4.2. Wage Differences by Race and Ethnicity in the Jasper Site, Cohort 1

Those working	Total (N = 31)	Black (N = 19)	White* (N = 12)
Average hourly wage	$6.56	$6.13	$7.23
Hours worked per week	33.8	34.7	32.3
Average years of education	11.5	12.2	10.5

*Includes Hispanic and other.
Source: Interviews with welfare leavers in Jasper, Texas, 1999.

of employees of the local cotton gin. They were working long hours every day. However, the cotton gin, they explained, was open only eight to ten weeks each year. Most of these temporary workers did not know where they would be working when their current jobs ended.

Other Sources of Income

Welfare leavers could not and did not depend solely on earned income. While most respondents did work, some respondents relied primarily on other sources of income. Welfare leavers often managed with the assistance of child support payments, spouses' earnings, and support from other family members.[2] In very few cases did families receive all of the money they needed from a single source. Usually households achieved their budgets through a fragmented and tenuous combination of strategies. Each income source contributed a part of what families needed to survive. However, some sources of income also placed additional constraints and demands on the family. Families getting assistance from relatives often needed to reciprocate with services needed by other family members. They often exchanged cash or services with others, who in turn helped them with transportation or food.

Child Support

Most families in our study relied on either earnings or TANF (and sometimes a combination of both for short periods, particularly if sporadic or off-the-books employment was included) as their primary sources of income. Although many mothers were eligible for monthly child support payments from a nonresidential parent, only 9 percent at the time of departure from TANF and 13 percent six months after leaving TANF received such support during the period of our study. The Texas Office of the Attorney General (OAG) is the state agency responsible for collecting and enforcing child support on behalf of custodial parents. Mothers on TANF were required to cooperate with the efforts of the OAG. However, if a mother was receiving a TANF cash allowance and the OAG received a child support payment on her behalf, she received only the first $50, while the state kept the remainder of the payment as reimbursement for her TANF payments. If the child support payment was more than $50 greater than the amount of the TANF grant over a sustained period of time, the family might lose their TANF benefit altogether. Custodial parents not receiving TANF were eligible to receive the entire child support payment without deduction.[3]

Administrative data tracked the receipts of child support obtained through the OAG. However, not all child support from low-income, nonresidential fathers was administered and tracked by the state.[4] Some parents made informal child support arrangements outside the official state channels. Indeed, a number of fathers made substantial nonfinancial contributions to their children, either in addition to or instead of cash payments.

According to administrative data tracking formal child support payments, among families who left TANF between April 1998 and June 1999, 7 percent received child support six months before leaving TANF, 9 percent received such support in the month they left, and 14 percent received it 18 months afterward (Figure 4.3).[5] The state agency had more time to work cases that remained on TANF, leading to improved rates over time for each cohort. Furthermore, collection rates have improved recently as a result of technological improvements in the collection and administration of child support payments. These changes included automatic wage-withholding collection procedures and the establishment of the National Directory of New Hires data system, a national system that tracks people beginning new jobs. The current national information base allows state offices to locate fathers working out-of-state and thereby increase the amount of their child support collections. Some of these improvements are reflected in the higher share of Cohort 2 TANF leavers who received child support payments. However, during the course of our study, the installation of the OAG's new computer system led to lengthy disruptions in child support payments to some families that had left TANF.[6]

Administrative data indicate that the average child support benefit received by a family that received any support at all in the month that the family left TANF was $207 ($232 for Cohort 2 leavers), and this amount increased modestly over time (Table 4.3). Twenty-one percent of families leaving TANF received at least one child support payment during the year after their exit from TANF. However, many welfare leavers we interviewed reported receiving only partial and irregu-

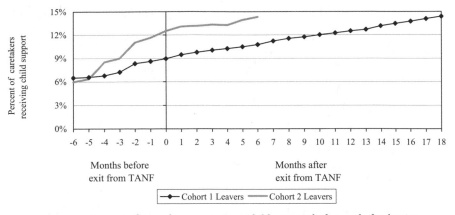

FIGURE 4.3. Percent of TANF leavers receiving child support before and after leaving TANF. Source: Administrative data from the Texas Department of Human Services and the Office of the Attorney General for cases leaving TANF from April 1998 through June 1999 (Cohort 1) or from July through September 2000 (Cohort 2).

Table 4.3. Child Support Outcomes for Cohort 1 TANF Leavers

	Percent of time monthly child support payments received	Mean dollar amount of monthly child support payments received*
6 months after exit	10.1%	$218
At exit	8.9%	$207
6 months before exit	6.9%	$138

*All dollar amounts are reported in constant year 2000 dollars.
Source: Administrative data from the Texas Department of Human Services and the Office of the Attorney General on those leaving TANF between April 1998 and June 1999.

lar child support payments. The statewide survey of TANF leavers reported that 19 percent of respondents had received child support sometime in the four to eight months after leaving TANF. Although informal payments were at times significant, they, like the more formal payments, were often very irregular.

In summary, the families we interviewed received child support in several different ways. In addition to state-supervised support, some mothers received cash payments directly from absent fathers, or, in a few cases, from relatives of the absent fathers. Others, while not receiving cash payments, received other kinds of important assistance from absent fathers and those fathers' families. Such assistance included buying diapers and formula, providing child care, and

· help with other needs, such as transportation. However, all levels of support might well be intermittent.

Although important, child support payments could not lift low-income mothers and their children out of poverty. Among fathers who paid child support, the irregular nature of many fathers' employment meant that those payments were inconsistent from month to month (see King and Schroeder, 2003, and Schroeder et al., 2004). And the payments themselves were rarely large enough to make a large difference in terms of the household budget.

Earned Income Tax Credit

The Urban Institute's National Survey of America's Families (NSAF), conducted in 1999, found that 74 percent of current welfare recipients in Texas and 80 percent of past recipients (a somewhat larger population than we studied) had heard of the EITC, even though only 33 percent of current and 69 percent of past recipients reported ever receiving it (Urban Institute, 2001b).[7] On the other hand, our statewide survey of TANF leavers found that only 3.3 percent of respondents reported using the EITC (24 out of 723 leavers) in the previous six months. However, most of our survey data were gathered more than six months after the previous tax filing deadline and before the post-TANF tax filing date; therefore, these figures may exclude some respondents who used the EITC in the previous tax year. However, these findings, along with research at a national level, suggest that only a small portion of recent TANF leavers in Texas benefit from the EITC.

Marriage

Welfare reform was designed to encourage two kinds of behavioral change in recipients by creating incentives to work and to marry. In our study, several women developed relationships with stably employed men that allowed them to leave welfare. However, marriage was the precipitating factor resulting in a woman's exit from welfare in only a handful of cases. Less than 9 percent of the TANF leavers in the administrative database were married while on TANF. (We are reluctant to report statistics on marriage from the phone-mail survey or the intensive interviews, since people described so many different relationship arrangements as marriage.) Only 4 percent of the survey respondents cited marriage as a contributing factor to leaving TANF within the past year. Even among the few cases we interviewed, only some marriages remained intact.

Table 4.4. Most Frequent Sources of Income and Economic Supports in Past Month, Cohort 2

Last month, did your household get income from . . .

Type of income received	Percentage of sample receiving	Dollar amount
Earnings from paid work	49.1%	$767
TANF	25.4%	$220
Child support	18.5%	$219
SSI Disability	10.0%	$552
Unemployment Benefits Insurance	4.7%	$451
Social Security Survivors	4.6%	$537

Source: Statewide survey of 723 families leaving TANF in July–September 2000.
Note: Families may have reported receiving income from multiple sources.

Total Family Income

In light of the variety of different income sources, calculating total household or family income was a difficult task. Most welfare leavers depended primarily on earned income, but earned income alone, even when household earnings were derived from the wages of multiple individuals, seldom met all the demands of even the most conservative household budget. Thus, earnings were often supplemented from a variety of other sources including non-TANF government benefits, child support, and EITC refunds, as well as gifts and contributions from partners, the fathers of children, and other family members.

Some sources of family income for TANF leavers could be accurately measured with administrative data. However, it was impossible even to estimate income from other sources using the data sources available for this study. Thus, the administrative data could not provide an accurate estimate of the total household income for many families.

In contrast to the administrative data, our statewide survey provided more detail about total household income. We asked respondents about their sources of income and other economic supports both in the past month and over the past six months. Nearly half of the sample reported earnings from paid work, while one-fourth received TANF because they had returned to the welfare rolls sometime after the departure that made them eligible for our study (Table 4.4). Nearly 19 percent received income from either formal or informal child support, while smaller groups received Social Security, ssi, and unemployment payments.

Earned income and TANF were the most frequent income sources reported by respondents. Many fewer respondents received income from unemployment insurance, ssi, worker's compensation, or the EITC. Some respondents cycled among jobs with periods of unemployment when they received TANF. In fact, a number of former TANF recipients either combined irregular or very low-paid work and TANF benefits or cycled between TANF and employment for their primary income sources.

In addition, several respondents reported improvements in their standards of living that did not result from changes in their income or marital or employment status. A younger woman who had begun receiving welfare as a runaway minor returned to live with her parents, who were economically comfortable and were now willing to support both her and her child. Another respondent received an unexpected inheritance. A few respondents left TANF when they began receiving a larger monthly allowance from ssi for chronic health conditions and disabilities. Additionally, a handful of respondents reported receiving Social Security survivors' benefits, and another very small group received Unemployment Insurance.

Altogether, employment was the most likely source of income for TANF leavers. However, like many of the other sources of income, both earned wages and TANF payments were relatively small and often irregular. Families also supported themselves through child support payments, assistance from other friends and relatives, and support from other government programs, including noncash supports such as Medicaid and food stamps that provided for important family needs. Overall, these families drew on multiple resources but still remained in poverty.

FIVE

Coping with Barriers to Self-Sufficiency

LUCIA WAS A twenty-five-year-old divorced mother of two boys, ages two and five. She earned a limited income in a low-wage job and could not afford the child care costs for two preschool boys. Lucia's family helped her with expenses by providing housing and child care at little or no cost, as well as assisting with her transportation needs. Despite her family's help, Lucia still found herself dealing with one crisis situation after another.

Lucia lived in a house her parents owned next door to the house in which she grew up. The rent was set at $200 a month, along with her promise to take care of the house, but she was seldom able to pay the rent. Lucia had earned her high school diploma and had begun college, planning to major in education and earn her teaching certification. However, Lucia left college when she became pregnant during her freshman year, and married soon thereafter. She enrolled in Temporary Assistance to Needy Families (TANF) when her husband left her with no car and a number of unpaid bills. Since becoming a single parent, she had received only two or three months of child support of about $250 a month. After receiving TANF aid, she went to work for a direct mail-order service, earning $6.00 an hour. During her first six months on the job, she was on probationary status with no benefits. Before Lucia could complete her probationary period and receive a scheduled raise, she was laid off, and she filed for unemployment.

When we met Lucia, she was working for a day-care center and was paid $5.75 an hour. Although the salary was low, she was able to support her children with the assistance she received from her family and others. A local community organization helped her with utilities for one month. Her mother and sister helped her with child care, for which she paid her mother $50 a week. When her mother was not available, other family members helped take care of her children.

Lucia had not owned her own car since her husband's departure, but she was able to use her brother's car to get to work. Even with her own transportation, work was a thirty-minute drive from her home. In exchange for use of the car, she assumed responsibility for the cost of car repairs and upkeep. When the car broke down, her brother or parents paid for the repairs, and Lucia paid them back. At the time of her interview, she owed her family $1,300 for car repairs. Fortunately, other family members lent her a different car to use during the times when her car was in the shop for repairs. After losing her Medicaid benefits when she left TANF, Lucia visited a local Planned Parenthood office, where she could receive a free annual physical examination. Her children retained their Medicaid coverage.

When emergencies did occur, Lucia relied on her family to pitch in. For instance, during the storm season the preceding year, the roof of her house collapsed, and her family repaired it. Even with significant support, however, she never seemed to keep pace with her expenses. In the six months preceding the interview, she had run out of food, her utilities and phone had been turned off, and she had been unable to find needed medical care.

Families leaving welfare often face a series of barriers that prevent them from sustaining employment. Ill health (Burton and Whitfield, 2003; Earle and Heymann, 2002; Heymann and Earle, 1999; Repetti et al., 1989), minimal access to reliable child care (Henly and Lyons, 2000), and poor job-related skills (Lane et al., 2001) are increasingly well-documented as barriers to sustained employment. Our research points to additional difficulties families experience finding and retaining employment because of problems with transportation, food shortages, and housing problems.

In our study, unemployed survey participants reporting any barriers cited an average of 2.3 different barriers to their employment, with one-third of the families (33 percent) reporting three or more barriers. The family interviews revealed that barriers were often interrelated. The presence of one barrier made it more difficult to respond to another barrier. The most prominent barriers (Table 5.1) were in the following areas:

- *Child Care.* Thirty-one percent of unemployed survey respondents reported problems affording child care in the preceding six months, which in turn interfered with working. According to the interview respondents, formal sector child care was unaffordable for most families who lacked child care subsidies. When informal child care arrangements were available for these families, the care was often unreliable.

- *Transportation.* Almost a quarter of all survey respondents (23 percent) and a slightly larger percentage of unemployed respondents (26 percent) had experienced employment-related problems caused by poor transportation in the preceding six months. Our in-person interviews indicated that difficulties with transportation affected not only employment but also access to other services and supports, including food stamps and Medicaid, particularly in rural areas, where people without a car often had trouble getting to agency offices to apply for services or to recertify for services already received.

- *Health Problems.* Some unemployed survey respondents reported health problems as precipitating employment loss (18 percent) and return to the TANF program (15 percent). With regard to overall health, 20 percent of all respondents reported a health problem or injury that interfered with their usual activities of daily living within the past six months, and 18 percent reported health problems among other family members during the same period. Our interviews with TANF leavers indicated that these health problems influenced respondents' employment options as they searched for new jobs.

Although the survey did not include specific questions about housing and food issues as barriers to employment, many respondents reported experiencing problems in those areas. Thirty-eight percent of survey respondents said that at some time during the previous six months, they had been unable to afford their housing costs. Thirty-seven percent also reported at least one occasion in the past six months when they needed food but could not afford to buy it. During the open-ended interviews, respondents explained that housing and food problems affected their employment options. Lacking stable sources of housing and food, respondents had difficulty being reliable employees, arriving on the job promptly and ready to work.

These problems affected respondents differently, depending on where in Texas they lived. Rural families experienced problems with health care and transportation differently than families in large urban areas. Without adequate transportation, rural families could not travel to search for work or work at the

Table 5.1. Barriers to Employment, Cohort 2

What are the main reasons why you are not working?

Total number of unemployed respondents: 385

Reason	No.	Percent
Child care problems	119	31.0%
Currently looking for work	103	26.8%
Transportation problems	98	25.5%
Own health problems	69	17.9%
Own physical or mental disabilities	44	11.4%
Could not find a job	43	11.2%
Other family members' health problems	38	9.9%

Source: Statewide survey of families leaving TANF in July–September 2000.

jobs they found. They were also limited in their ability to travel to education and training programs, child care facilities, and health care providers. In many rural counties, as in the two where we conducted open-ended interviews, public transportation was not available at all. On the other hand, in large metropolitan areas, such as Houston and San Antonio, most families had some access to transportation, yet daily work commutes of several hours on public transportation were not uncommon. Urban families described weighing the costs and problems with public transportation against their need for the goods or services to which the transportation gave them access. For instance, a commute might bring them to a large chain grocery store with lower prices than the smaller neighborhood store, but the travel was costly in time and money.

Families in large urban areas also experienced food shortages and insecurity and housing problems differently than did rural families. Where rural families occasionally hunted and grew their own food, urban families had to buy all their food, unless it was given to them. In both urban and rural sites, however, families described food shortages at the end of the month, and days when they did not know where the next day's food was coming from (one definition of food insecurity).

Families we interviewed in urban areas often described being evicted from their homes or becoming nearly homeless. In such circumstances, they moved in with relatives or, less often, friends. If all else failed, they applied to home-

less shelters. Rural families faced the prospect of homelessness with fewer available resources since there were few shelters or other service organizations in
rural areas. In one rural area, three adult siblings had all been evicted from their
homes within a few months of each another. When we interviewed them, they
were all living together in a single rental unit and expected eviction in the next
few weeks. They had no plans for that eventuality.

Thus, many families faced different and often multiple barriers to economic
self-sufficiency. However, there were important relationships among the barriers
that an individual family faced. Families explained how one employment barrier
might exacerbate the impact of a different employment barrier. For instance, a
lack of transportation created additional barriers to accessing child care, and
the combination of the two made it even more unlikely that the parent could
find and retain a job. The relationships among multiple barriers were complex
and often synergistic, exacerbating the effect of each individual barrier and creating an interference with employment greater than the sum of the individual
barriers.

Coping Strategies

When neither government services nor earned income provided sufficient
means, families turned to their communities and to informal supports. As reported in earlier work (Edin and Lein, 1997), strategies used by families to garner
resources and sustain employment included (1) getting assistance from family
and friends for help with transportation, child care, food, housing, and other
items, (2) finding irregular jobs or second jobs, and (3) getting assistance from
local agencies. Overall, family and friends provided help with transportation,
child care, food, housing, and other items for our survey TANF leavers (Table
5.2).

Child Care

One-third of all survey respondents experienced problems with child care in
the six months preceding our interviews. Thirty-one percent of unemployed respondents identified child care as contributing to their problems finding and
keeping employment. Only a small fraction of the families we spoke to used
formal child care arrangements, and an almost identical fraction received support from the state Child Care Management System (CCMS) (recently reorga-
nized and renamed the Child Care Management Services agencies). Less than
20 percent of the families used care by nonrelatives at all. A small minority of

Table 5.2. Assistance from Family and Friends, Cohort 2

In the past six months, have family or friends helped you with . . .

Total number of respondents: 723

Type of assistance from family and friends if informant responded "Frequently" or "Sometimes"

Transportation	43.7%
Child care	34.1%
Food	28.2%
Housing	26.3%
Bills	26.0%
Household items	23.0%
Clothing	20.1%

Source: Statewide survey of families leaving TANF in July–September 2000.

families, 10 percent, left older children (usually older than nine or ten years) to care for themselves. Respondents were most likely to care for their children themselves or to enlist the help of relatives (Table 5.3).

Each of these strategies had implications for both children and parents. They either improved or undermined a parent's ability to secure employment over the long term. Because affordable child care was such a scarce resource, many families varied their strategies over time, depending on their current situational needs and resources. Families also coped by using multiple strategies at a time.

CARE PROVIDED BY PARENTS

Welfare leavers tended to care for their own children during periods of unemployment or when they were able to rely on a spouse or partner as the primary wage earner. However, caring for one's children actively interfered with employment or job search activities. Some families managed to care for their older children on their own, restricting their work hours to school hours. A few parents had part-time jobs they could do at home or were allowed to bring a child to their workplace. Unfortunately, when child care arrangements failed or a child became ill, parents often faced a significant loss of pay and risked losing their jobs through having to care for the child. Mothers felt particularly torn about leaving very young children for long periods.

Table 5.3. Child Care Strategies, Cohort 2

*How do you take care of your youngest child when you are working/
at school/have to be away from home? (✓ all that apply)*

Total number of respondents: 723

I take care of my child myself	25.8%
Child at babysitter/nonrelative cares for child at that person's home	7.4%
Other parent takes care of child	11.4%
Child old enough to care for self	9.4%
Child in after-school program	4.2%
Older sibling takes care of child	7.8%
Other relative takes care of child in my home	17.3%
Other relative takes care of child somewhere else	15.5%
Child in day care at a child care center or family day care home	13.7%
Other	11.7%

Source: Statewide survey of families leaving TANF in July–September 2000.

I read that where this age, between one and two, is really a good age for you to be home with them also. I've really tried taking jobs that I can stay home with her as much as possible.

CARE PROVIDED BY RELATIVES

When relatives lived in close proximity, extended family members often assisted with child care. Thus, many TANF leavers depended on their parents for child care. TANF parents often felt their children were safer in the loving care of grand-parents than in formal care, which they saw as potentially risky to their children's safety and well-being.

At first I had a lot of problems finding a babysitter, but my mom was always there.... So I guess I could say she was a person I could fall back on. She was the only person, because other than her—I mean, if I didn't have my mother, I guess I couldn't, you know, I couldn't count on anybody else. Because I mean—there's so many things that you hear in the news that men molest children and so forth—and then a lot of things happen in day cares too, you know, that the child caretakers, that they hurt the kids and stuff, so I never put my daughter in a day care. I never did. My mom always helped me with that. So I guess I'm lucky in that part.

When children were too young to be on their own and mothers had to work, relatives often filled in gaps in the availability of child care, as mothers scheduled work hours around their children's needs and relatives' availability.

When we talked about child care and other issues, families themselves reflected widely prevalent cultural beliefs that women in ethnic minority enclaves have more access than other women to help from extended family networks (Uttal, 1997, 1999). One mother whose husband is of Mexican heritage depended on her in-laws to care for the children on weekends:

> Hopefully they'll give me a break. They [children] usually go every weekend because she [mother-in-law] is off on the weekends. I don't want to sound like funny when I say this, but they say that people that are from Mexico, they're like more into families. They always want to be with their family, and you know, so, my grandparents they're from here, all of my family's from here. And they're like, "No, no, I can't take care of them. No I can't do this, no I can't do that." But every Friday as soon as she [mother-in-law] gets home she calls me, "Can I pick up the kids so they can come over?" You know, it's like she's real.

Mothers, grandmothers, aunts, and other relatives, usually female, were an invaluable resource. However, because of sometimes complex individual family dynamics, depending on relatives was not always easy. Some parents found it quite difficult to turn to their own parents for assistance:

> Especially if you never get along with them. Well, my dad, he's easy to get along with. My mom, ever since I remember, I've never gotten along with her. And, then brothers, sometimes . . . It's me, then him, then my baby brother. The one in the middle, sometimes he tries to, like, tell my kids, you know, yell at them or whatever, something like that. And I don't like it. I don't like anybody getting after my kids. I think I get after them, you know, enough. It's hard.

Other parents lost child care assistance when grandparents or great-aunts become too ill to continue to care for children. On still other occasions, relatives themselves returned to work and were no longer available as a child care resource.

OTHER CARETAKER OPTIONS

Mothers without strong family networks who were responsible for young children turned to other people for child care assistance. However, mothers usually drew on such assistance only for short periods of time; they were by nature temporary arrangements. Friends and neighbors had their own children and jobs, and often their own extended families. While they could help out on occasion, they usually could not provide full-time, reliable child care or care over a long period of time. One respondent explained that while a friend helped her out with child care, she had to rely on herself most of the time.

> I have a girlfriend of mine; her daughter is sixteen. She'll come over and sit with them, you know, something like that. Or I'll get a friend to sometimes, but usually I take them everywhere with me. It gets real stressful.

CHILDREN'S SELF-CARE

Mothers who could not afford or who were distrustful of the child care system and who had few informal supports trained their children at relatively early ages to care for themselves.

> Before I used to work graveyard, so my mom used to take care of them at night, and during the day I was at home for them. So I really didn't have [formal child care], but right now one's twelve and one's ten, so I go in at 7 o'clock in the morning, get out at 3:30, so they only stay here about an hour by themselves, but they're big enough. They know you aren't supposed to open the door. So I just come and they're inside; they don't even go outside. And I have a phone and I call them up and check up on them.

While few parents left their children without adult supervision, some parents expected their children to function with considerable independence when the parents were sleeping, shopping, or caring for other children. One respondent explained how her children were trained to be safe and remain home so she could nap in between work and home responsibilities:

> But you know what, though, I can go to sleep and come back, and they'll just be laying here looking at TV. They don't get into anything. Like you would think little kids would mess with this or that, what I started doing was putting tape over something, and when they went by it, they knew it was a no-no, they knew it was a no-no, so I never had any problem with them getting into anything. Now kids are going to make a mess, true, but I don't worry about, you know, them getting hurt or anything because—well, they did break my glass table—that's why the chairs are just sitting there, they broke my glass table. But other than that, they're just being bored. You know, they'll play by themselves, and sometimes they'll fight like little boys do, and that's it.

In only a few cases did mothers leave children home alone. These parents depended on their children to remain in the house, keep themselves safe, and stay out of trouble. For those living in more dangerous neighborhoods, children were often instructed to stay inside the house with the windows closed and the doors locked.

FORMAL CARE

Relatively few families used formal care, and they depended on subsidized care, usually through what was at the time the state's CCMS, to afford it. However, as family members pointed out to us, while such care was valuable and reliable when they had it, it disappeared when they lost the subsidy. Families lost their child care subsidy if they did not meet work requirements, if they had been off TANF for a considerable length of time, or if they were judged not to have used the child care effectively. In some cases, families lost their child care subsidy after an extended illness-related absence of a child because they were considered ineffective users of the benefit.

Transportation

Twenty-three percent of all survey respondents and a slightly larger proportion of unemployed respondents (26 percent) reported that lack of transportation had interfered with their employment during the past six months. Just over half of the employed survey respondents reported using their own car to get to work. Other respondents borrowed cars, drove with other people, used public transportation, or walked. However, in more rural areas, it was likely that the only potential transportation was a family car.

Rural respondents became even more isolated without transportation and found their access to other services and supports, including food stamps and Medicaid, restricted. In rural areas, some households without transportation were unable to visit health care providers even if they had Medicaid coverage. For instance, in Jasper County, where there was no public transportation system and only one taxicab, respondents traveled up to fifty miles round-trip to jobs and potential jobs. They traveled similar distances to welfare offices to apply and recertify for food stamps and Medicaid. It was impossible for respondents to keep appointments with the welfare office, attend job training and placement, apply for jobs, or sustain employment without access to a reliable car. Many of them lost jobs and benefits when their transportation failed.

Particularly in rural areas, respondents felt acutely vulnerable to unemployment as well as family emergencies without access to a reliable car. They could not get to work or meet sudden family needs without a car. Families with children, especially those dealing with health problems, were concerned about having transportation in the event of a sudden health crisis.

My oldest son has started having epileptic seizures again. It has been three years since his last seizure. The doctor told us that he has a spot on his brain that gets bigger every time he has a seizure. Today, the school took my son to the hospital since I didn't have the transportation to pick him up from school.

At the same time, respondents were discouraged by welfare caseworkers from applying for public services if they owned a car, and understood that they might be disqualified for some benefits if they owned a car above a certain value. In contrast, the two urban sites reported the lowest level of car ownership. Urban respondents also repeatedly mentioned that car ownership caused them to be ineligible for TANF and other services. However, these eligibility rules were especially difficult for rural respondents, who felt caught in a system that was punitive toward car ownership, even though a car was necessary to meet the new TANF guidelines, which emphasized active employment searches, job training, and transition to work.

Because automobiles were so vital for family survival in some areas, family members sometimes co-signed loans and titles to enable another family member to purchase a car. The cosignature on a car note could potentially disqualify an individual for public assistance, particularly if an individual had co-signed on more than one note. In one household, the father who was employed in a relatively stable (although low-wage) job had co-signed on several car loans to help his children buy cars. When this information surfaced during the process of applying for assistance, the father was denied benefits because he exceeded the asset criteria.

Transportation problems further increased respondents' vulnerability even as they attempted to meet the demands of the welfare system to attend training and attend eligibility and recertification meetings. Mothers without cars depended on friends and relatives for rides or the loan of the car. Even so, such transportation often fell short, as rural respondents in particular described missed appointments and penalties when their transportation arrangements failed.

We were required to go up to the Texas Workforce Commission for some kind of training and I had my car back then, and I was going to pick up a friend of mine (and you know so far out of town) and I had a flat tire and we finally got the tire fixed and stuff and by the time I got my tire fixed, I headed straight down there to let them know that I had a flat tire and stuff because I didn't have no way of calling them and let them know I was going to be late. So by the time I got up there it was too late to get in the class, and they penalized me [a provision of the personal responsibility agreement that all TANF recipients signed in order to get benefits]. I've been down there several times to ask her when's the next class, and she said it was going to be the next month but they never did set me up another appointment. For the next month, I was calling to ask about the next class and they never could give me an answer.... I asked my caseworker would it do me any good to fight it and stuff and he told me no.... He was the one that told me that I had to take the class.... I thought maybe they could work something out with me because I was willing to take the class and stuff. I want to learn where I could go back to school or that they could help train me to where I could get a better job and all this stuff.... I guess I just try to live day to day as it comes. I just try not to worry about it.

Respondents to the statewide survey indicated that family and friends were often a source of transportation. Forty-four percent of the respondents received what they considered frequent assistance with transportation during the preceding six months. At the other end of the spectrum, more than a third of the survey respondents (38.2 percent) had not received any help with transportation from family or friends. Even for those without other options, relying on others for rides was a relatively unreliable strategy. For these respondents, transportation became contingent on a number of related factors, including the health of the person providing transportation, the condition of the car, and an ongoing good relationship between the respondent and car owner. Changes in any of these factors placed the respondent's access to transportation at risk.

Health Problems

Some unemployed survey respondents reported experiencing health problems that resulted in loss of employment (18 percent) or a return to the TANF program (15 percent), or both. A fifth of all respondents (20 percent) reported experiencing a health problem or injury that interfered with daily activities, and a similar proportion (18 percent) reported that family members were experiencing health problems.[1] Further, our family interviews indicated that these health problems in turn affected families' employment options. Almost half of those who returned to the TANF program cited their own poor health or that of a family member as the primary cause for their return. Twenty percent of survey respondents reported that they had a health problem or injury that kept them from "doing things that people generally do." Eighteen percent of survey respondents reported that someone in the household had a disability or health problems that made it difficult for the respondent to go to work. If respondents didn't have Medicaid, or if they needed a service not covered by Medicaid, they often went without health care.

Families described the ways in which health conditions could precipitate a return to TANF. Some leavers returned because their health conditions prevented them from performing well on the job. More typically, however, health problems limited the number of hours and types of activities a respondent could perform at work.

> I cannot work sitting down, which is telemarketing. I learned my computers, I was all excited. I graduated, I was there on time every day, I took the bus, I asked for rides, but I did it. I graduated; they even gave me bonuses on my checks, because I was doing so well, and all of a sudden this just, you know, it just came back and I got sick again. So that is the reason I'm in and out of TANF again, you know.

Some respondents who struggled with chronic illness while they continued to work found they could not meet the demands of their employment without putting their health at greater risk.

> I'm anemic. And I helped them out a lot like they would go . . . Oh, so-and-so didn't come in; can you cover for them. I'm like, "Sure." So I was like throwing in like doubles daily and like I usually eat but since they had called me early in the morning, they're like, can you come in because they like didn't come in. So, I woke up, took a shower and left, and I wasn't able to eat. So, since I'm a anemic, I was working on an empty stomach. I started getting sick and started blacking out. . . . I like told them, "Can I have a ten-minute break?" and they're like, "No." I said, "I'm not asking to smoke a cigarette. I'm not asking to go get on the phone. I'm asking to eat a taco sitting down without running back and forth to customers." I was a waitress . . . just want to sit down for ten minutes eating a taco so this can pass. And they're like, "Who in the hell told you that you can have a ten-minute break?" And I was like . . . "I need a ten-minute break. I told you my condition." I just like said "I'm sorry," and just walked out. I called my aunt. She said, "I know that condition you get. I know how sick you are when you do get sick. I will come pick you up in five minutes." I was like, "I am going to lose my job." She's like, "Losing your job is better than your son losing you."

The people we met, particularly those off welfare and working, were often caught in a conundrum. They needed health insurance in order to receive medical treatment, and the medical treatment was often a necessary prerequisite to their ability to work. On the other hand, they were ineligible for public medical care programs and could not acquire health insurance privately. In some cases, repeated changes in respondents' health insurance status as the person cycled on and off TANF meant that medical treatment that began while a respondent was insured might stop, sometimes abruptly, if that insurance coverage ended. Respondents reported stopping medical treatment in mid-course, as in the case of a woman who had her tooth extracted but went without the follow-up dental care to replace the tooth, which would have maintained the arrangement of teeth in her mouth and provided a better appearance:

> When I was working, I was planning on going to a dentist. I had to go get a tooth pulled [before I had health insurance] in front, and you know it kind of made me feel, it bothers me and stuff when I can't get teeth replaced. I don't like to smile. . . . It bothers me. I don't like to smile.

To meet family needs, respondents either did without health care services or tried to purchase them outside the regular system. Households on the Texas-Mexico border often purchased medical care and medications in Mexico, where they could afford them. Although this strategy allowed parents to affordably attend to urgent health problems, families were sometimes violating United States laws. Unable to obtain local public health care for her children, as a last resort, one respondent went to Mexico to get antibiotics without a prescription.

> I finally received word about the Texas Healthy Kids program. They put my kids on a waiting list. They said that funds for this area were not available at this time. So my kids, except the baby, are still uninsured. My son is sick right now. He has a very high fever. I just put him to bed. One of my girls got sick last week. She had swollen tonsils. I had to take her to the doctor. I paid $40 for the visit. The doctor prescribed an antibiotic for her, but when he found out that I didn't have any insurance he changed the antibiotic to a cheaper one; the first one would have cost me $60. Now my oldest daughter is sick. She stayed home from school today. She has a fever and other symptoms. I bought some medicine from Mexico for her that my sister told me about. I think I might have to start buying them medicine in Mexico when they get sick. I think I'm going to get my son's antibiotics from there. Last time we went through several antibiotics until we finally found one that would cure his ear infection.

In some cases when respondents could not get the care they needed for themselves or their children, the health problem precipitated a return to TANF. These respondents saw welfare as the only route for acquiring needed medical services and knew they would also receive at least minimal financial support when either caregiving or their own incapacity kept them from working. One respondent described using TANF to support her family while she negotiated a worker's compensation claim for a job-related injury.

> I was working at a motel and I hurt myself on the job and that was in April. That's the only reason I'm on TANF right now is because of my back injury and stuff and [points to the medication she was taking] so I can't do too much of anything right now anyways. So I'm trying, in order for me to make it and stuff I have to go down there and apply for [TANF] until I find out what's going to happen on my worker's comp.

Especially in rural areas, but also in the larger cities, respondents found that the travel and waiting time involved in accessing medical care might interfere with their employment. Respondents using clinics and emergency rooms often waited most of the day for treatment. When caring for a family member with intensive medical needs, many respondents found it impossible to continue working, and as a result some returned to TANF.

> I explained to my social worker that I had to be constantly driving around because I'd take my dad to dialysis four times a week and I had problems driving and had no one to help me. She checked my file and said I qualified for benefits.

Housing and Food

Housing and food problems usually are not considered barriers to employment. However, our respondents not only reported many episodes of difficulties in both areas but explained how both housing and food difficulties made it hard to find and keep a job. Stable housing remained a particularly acute problem for a sizable minority of welfare leavers. In fact, 37 percent of survey respondents reported that at some time over the preceding six months they could not afford their housing (Table 5.4). Almost 40 percent of the survey respondents also reported having lived with family or friends over the preceding six months until they could find affordable housing of their own. Smaller proportions of respondents experienced evictions, lived in emergency housing, or found themselves without any shelter at all.

Table 5.4. Incidence of Housing Problems in Past Six Months

Over the past 6 months, has there been a time when:

Total number of survey respondents: 723

Type of housing problem	Share of total respondents
You could not afford a place to stay or when you could not pay your rent?	37.3%
You were evicted from any residence?	8.5%
You lived in emergency housing shelter or domestic violence shelter?	3.6%
You were homeless or living on the street or in a car?	4.6%
You lived with family or friends until you could get your own place?	38.4%
You have been without electricity because you could not afford it?	15.8%
You have been without heat because you could not afford it?	16.6%

Source: Statewide survey of families leaving TANF in July–September 2000

When family members unexpectedly lost jobs, their housing was often jeopardized as well. Because Texas is a state with few legal protections for tenants, eviction proceedings might be concluded in a matter of weeks, leaving families scrambling for a place to live. The families we interviewed also experienced eviction when their housing was condemned. Low-income tenants who lived in substandard housing that required extensive rehabilitation were often summarily asked to leave during the repair process.

Families engaged in several different strategies to cope with a sudden loss of housing. Some families moved into homeless shelters. In some cases, emergency homeless shelters appeared to be a family's only option. In other cases, families voluntarily chose to live in shelters, knowing their need would be given a high priority and they would go to the head of the waiting list for entry into public housing.

Homeless families also moved in with others, usually with relatives. While providing an immediate short-term housing solution, this doubling-up often created new problems. Host relatives in public housing violated their lease by allowing other family members to share their housing. As a result, both families could be evicted when the arrangement was discovered. Relatives who them-

selves were living in impoverished conditions and the families who moved in
with them frequently ended up living in very crowded conditions. In some cases,
a mother and several children shared a single room or lived in a garage behind
the house.

Poor housing also contributed to substandard living conditions that negatively affected families' lives and health in different ways. In a few homes, families lived with no internal kitchen facilities, no plumbing, and no flooring. According to our respondents, some landlords knew their renters had few options
and failed to adequately maintain the housing they rented out. One respondent
described a situation where the landlord's inaction led to real consequences for
low-income tenants living in his apartment complex.

> The sewers backed up some time last year. And there was a hepatitis out-
> break in the apartment complex because they took forever to fix it. And I'm
> not trying to be mean, but some of the people that live there do not take
> care of their kids right. Their children were playing in sewage. That's sick-
> ening. . . . We reported it to the apartment complex. And they had to fix it
> because it was on their property. It wasn't the city's thing. But the city did
> come out to try to help them. They had it like that for so long there was a
> hepatitis outbreak.

Families who experienced housing problems explained the difficulties inherent in finding and keeping a job while living in insecure or inadequate housing.
As employees or potential employees, respondents understood the importance
of maintaining acceptable hygiene and a professional appearance. They also
needed to be well rested to be successful on the job. Furthermore, many workers
and job seekers needed regular access to a telephone.

Some housing difficulties, like many other problems, reflected the unique
issues arising in rural areas, where substandard housing was often outside town
limits and few public housing units had ever been built. Remote homesteads
in rural areas might lack utilities, plumbing, modern cooking appliances, and
heat. There were fewer available emergency housing resources, such as shelters.
One household we interviewed consisted of three families living together in one
small isolated house.

Except when adult children moved back with their parents, doubling-up
rarely provided a long-term solution to housing problems. As several respondents noted, too few bathrooms created difficulties for all in the household to get
ready for jobs and school at the same time. In addition, without access to a telephone, employers and potential employers could not easily contact respondents
about jobs or notify them about changes in hours or shifts.

Thirty-seven percent of the survey respondents reported that on at least one occasion over the preceding six months they needed food but couldn't afford to purchase it. Furthermore, 21 percent of respondents reported having gone hungry during the same period. Whether wages or food stamps were a household's primary means for getting food, by the end of the month, resources were often running low. As they approached the end of each month, most low-income families' diets changed, as the types of food they could afford became less varied and the number of meals per day was sometimes reduced from three to two. In urban areas, families went to available food pantries when they could; however, agencies also had restrictions on the number of visits each household could make to the food pantry.

In more rural areas, families who gardened and hunted expanded their food reserves. However, both gardening and hunting required access to specific resources of land, supplies, and skills. Rural families that lacked either these resources or assistance from community organizations might be uncertain at times about how to provide their children's next meal.

As with other barriers, food insecurity interfered with the ability to be a productive and reliable worker. Obtaining food stamps and accessing food pantries usually took time away from work. The food stamp program required in-person visits for eligibility confirmation and recertification. Food pantries were open only during set hours, typically during the day. Many parents responded to food shortages by skipping meals themselves so that their children could eat. Consequently, respondents were less alert and energetic and experienced hunger when they were at work.

More than a quarter of the survey respondents (28 percent) turned to family and friends for assistance with food frequently or some of the time. However, the family interviews revealed considerable variation in the patterns that families used to get needed household food. Some respondents received regular food assistance from family, such as one respondent who reported that on most weekends she went to her mother's home for food. Other households received assistance only during emergencies. For instance, one respondent's family pitched in when her food stamps were unaccountably delayed.

Multiple Barriers

On average, unemployed survey participants reporting barriers cited at least two different barriers to employment, and one-third mentioned three or more barriers. During the qualitative interviews, respondents described how the existence of one barrier made it more difficult to cope with other barriers. The interviews revealed that long-term difficulties finding and sustaining employment often resulted from a multiplicity of ongoing barriers. Respondents with multiple barriers to employment had the greatest difficulties in achieving long-term self-sufficiency. For instance, a respondent might explain that she was unemployed because she couldn't find work yet. Later in the interview, she might add that she had difficulty finding work because of her poor health. In the course of describing reasons for not working, another respondent revealed additional barriers to employment, beyond the lack of necessary skills: lack of child care and inadequate transportation:

> The self-sufficiency program caseworker told me I had to make an application for office work, but I had to type forty-five words a minute. I can only type thirty-five. And they have a school there . . . so you can practice everyday, but I don't have anyone to watch my kids. So it's holding me back. I know there's a job right there waiting for me, but it keeps holding me back. . . . I want to get a job where I can afford my kids, my shoes, clothes. . . . I want someone to get me a good car because my car is falling apart already. I can't drive my car at night because there are no lights. . . . So I want a car, and whatever happens, I buy a car then they take away my food stamps. . . . And I can't get on a bus; I've got five kids. And the bus is expensive. . . . I don't feel like anything is going my way.

Another woman expressed similar frustrations in her attempts to find steady employment. She also pointed out employment problems created by multiple barriers.

> I'm looking for jobs. I went through the paper. I went to four or five places a day putting in job applications. But everywhere I went, they told me the hours we're looking for is night or evening time. But I needed day hours. I needed maybe 8 to 2. That way I could take my son to school about 7:30 and then pick him up after school. A lot of places, they aren't hiring for that. They were hiring for early morning or evening. . . .

When asked about transportation, the woman continued:

> I've been asking their father [the father of her children] if I can use his mother's credit. Because I know as soon as I get a car and I find day care, I can have a job. But you need one thing to do another thing.

Another respondent reported complicated reasons for not working, related to her restricted access to public services when she was employed.

> The day care, the transportation, the hours. I need to make sure that I'm within my boundaries that I can work. . . . I can't work at [name of company]

because usually what they're hiring right now is second shift from three to twelve. I don't have anybody to take care of my kids. I just don't leave them with anybody. So what can I do? I can't find a job that will get me during the day time and even if I did, it would only be thirty hours a week. I can live off of it but they take that bit away that I need every month just to help pay two or three bills. They raise my rent, they lower my stamps, they take everything off. . . .

Facing Barriers to Work

In some ways, the survey provided a static view of the exigencies faced by low-income households after they left welfare. However, what we learned from both the administrative data and the intensive interviews is that most families experienced welfare receipt as part of a more dynamic process in which families regularly cycled through periods of hardship. The administrative data confirmed that families cycled on and off TANF as well as other antipoverty programs. The intensive interviews helped us understand how issues related to housing, food, and health contributed to general family instability and patterns of cycling. We began with Lucia's story, which illustrated how even employed families with relative stability one year may find themselves facing additional problems and instability the next. Thus, the percentages of families experiencing problems that we have reported are likely to underestimate the likelihood that a family will face a given hardship over a more extended time period. In the next chapter, we examine the ways in which the problems facing families leaving welfare interrelate, as well as their relationships to employment and return to TANF.

SIX

Staying Employed and Off Welfare

IN THIS CHAPTER, we step back from families' personal accounts to take a broader look at the factors affecting whether families ultimately succeed or fail after TANF benefits have ended. We first report the number of families who left TANF only to return to the welfare rolls within six months of leaving, and we describe who these families tended to be. Then we examine the reasons why families left TANF and got jobs, only to return to welfare. We obtained information on these issues in two ways: by surveying families directly and by developing regression models that used both the survey responses and the social service agencies' records to identify the most important patterns among recipients' histories. This approach helped us pinpoint which among the many complex factors in these families' lives contributed the most to their ultimate economic success or failure in life after welfare.

Low-wage families are challenged to find a job not only with stable income but also with adequate benefits, such as health insurance, to support families during emergencies. TANF leavers' first jobs are often short-term and irregular. They have few, if any, benefits, and because these jobs are often characterized by irregular hours, dependence on tips, or piece-rate work, the pay is also irregular. Therefore, TANF is frequently the only option for families when jobs fail them or

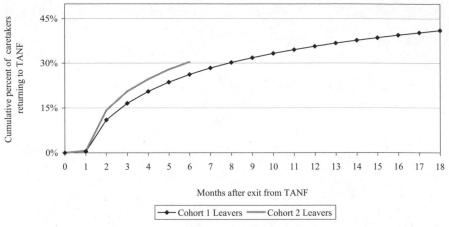

FIGURE 6.1.   Return of welfare leavers to TANF. Source: Administrative data from the
Texas Department of Human Services for cases leaving TANF from April 1998 through
June 1999 (Cohort 1) or from July through September 2000 (Cohort 2).

those they depend on, or when they need benefits that the jobs do not provide.
The families in our study (or, in Figure 6.1, the adult caretakers of young children) were most likely to return to TANF in the first few months after leaving the
program, with 28 percent returning to welfare within the first six months after
they left (Figure 6.1). Over the eighteen-month follow-up period, 41 percent of
families returned to TANF at some time, although many left again during the
observation period.[1]

     Our study included two cohorts of families in which both the parent and the
children left TANF. We were able to track families from the first cohort, families
who left TANF between April 1998 and June 1999, for eighteen months, a period
of time long enough to allow us to differentiate between those families who were
able to stay off TANF for at least six months and those who returned to TANF during the first six months. Understanding these families' histories can contribute to
the goals of understanding the cycles and rhythms in the lives of impoverished
families and designing policies that better assist families to make more stable
and lasting transitions from welfare to the workforce.

     Families that returned to TANF within six months after leaving welfare dif-
fered from other TANF leaver families in a number of ways. The heads of these
families were disproportionately Black, tended to be young, less than twenty-
five years old, had not completed high school, and were responsible for three or
more children. These recipients also reported greater utilization of government
services than other leavers, had lower incomes when they worked, and had spent

less time in the labor force. Table 6.1 outlines the differences between short-term leavers and other leavers in more detail.

Why Families Leave TANF

Approximately 16 percent of families on welfare left TANF during each month of the study, a somewhat higher rate than in the pre–welfare reform era.[2] We used two different methods—regression analyses with administrative data only and analysis of survey results—to find out why families left TANF. First, we surveyed the second cohort of families. Second, since agency (or administrative) data for both cohorts were available on families over a longer time period, we were able to construct regression equations that measured which family characteristics were most related to families leaving and remaining off TANF. We also listened to what families themselves had to say and used their accounts to illustrate the more quantitative analyses.

What Families Told Us

In our survey, we asked families why they left TANF. In four of every ten families, the interviewees reported leaving welfare either because they had a job or because their family earned too much money. (Because of the extremely low level of welfare benefits in Texas, just about any job that lasted a few months would have sufficed to make a family ineligible for cash assistance.) However, almost 60 percent of families left TANF for a wide range of non-employment-related reasons (Table 6.2). Generally, these reasons lined up under two broad themes: families began receiving income from sources other than their own jobs (such as through child support, marriage, or money from other adults) or they had difficulty dealing with the rules and administration of TANF and related systems.

Some women opted out of the TANF program when they could not or would not meet the requirement to provide information about their children's fathers. Several survey respondents explained that their children's fathers provided considerable support, but the women needed them to do so in a way that wouldn't count against their welfare benefits. Between the limited TANF benefits and low-income fathers' limited ability to help out, the mother needed both resources to make ends meet. Furthermore, mothers who had amicable agreements with fathers to provide informal support were often unwilling to implicate (and perhaps alienate) the father. They felt it was not worth disrupting arrangements they had with the fathers of their children, particularly since the state system would apply most of the father's payments to reimbursing the welfare benefit, leaving

Table 6.1. Demographic Characteristics of Short-Term and Long-Term TANF Leavers, Cohort 1

	Total sample (Cohort 1) (N = 143,500 families)	Short-term leavers: Returned to TANF within 6 months (N = 34,510 families)	Long-term leavers: Still off TANF after 6 months (N = 108,990 families)
Age of caretaker			
Average age (yr)	29.9	29.3	30.1
18–25	38.1%	41.7%	37.0%
26–34	34.4%	33.7%	34.6%
35–44	20.0%	17.9%	20.7%
≥45	7.5%	6.8%	7.7%
Race of caretaker			
Black	29.4%	34.3%	27.9%
Hispanic	45.2%	44.4%	45.4%
White	24.5%	20.6%	25.7%
Other	0.9%	0.7%	1.0%
Caretaker's educational level			
No high school education	16.4%	17.8%	15.9%
Some high school education	33.4%	37.8%	32.0%
Graduated from high school (or GED)	50.3%	44.5%	52.1%
Geography			
Urban—county with large MSA	52.4%	51.4%	52.7%
Suburban—county with other MSA	27.4%	26.9%	27.5%
Rural—county with no MSA	20.2%	21.7%	19.8%
Caretaker work history			
Percent time employed in prior 2 years	38.8%	35.9%	39.7%
Type of family			
Single-parent families	91.1%	92.4%	90.6%
Two-parent families	8.9%	7.6%	9.4%

Table 6.1. *Continued*

	Total sample (Cohort 1) (N = 143,500 families)	Short-term leavers: Returned to TANF within 6 months (N = 34,510 families)	Long-term leavers: Still off TANF after 6 months (N = 108,990 families)
Number of children			
Average number of children	2.0	2.1	2.0
Families with one child	41.0%	37.6%	42.1%
Families with two children	31.3%	31.2%	31.4%
Families with three or more children	27.6%	31.2%	26.5%
Ages of children			
Average age of youngest child (yr)	4.7	4.3	4.9
Average age of all children (yr)	6.2	5.9	6.3

Source: Administrative data on those leaving TANF between April 1998 and June 1999.

the mother with less money coming into her household. One woman explained that, owing to the presence in her household of·her boyfriend (who was also the father of her children), her TANF grant had been reduced. However, she pointed out that, as she understood the rules, if he didn't live with her, the state would pursue him for child support, and then keep most of the child support it received as reimbursement for the woman's TANF. She argued, and many women agreed, that you can receive financial assistance from your children's father and still need financial help from the state.

Other respondents lost benefits because of agency denials due to procedural mix-ups. Several said that they had been unable to keep appointments; others reported receiving appointment letters after a scheduled appointment at the welfare office. A common reason cited by respondents for missing the orientation sessions required by the welfare office was their inability to arrange child care. Other respondents commented that appointments often conflicted with work responsibilities: they had to choose between keeping the appointment at the wel-

Table 6.2. Reasons for Leaving TANF, Cohort 2

For everyone:
Why did you go off TANF the last time that happened?
(✓ all that apply):

Total number of respondents: 723

Found a job/income too high	41.4%
Another adult contributed money	10.0%
Began receiving child support	8.9%
Couldn't meet TANF requirements	7.5%
Reached TANF/welfare time limit*	6.6%
Could not get to required meetings/appointments	6.5%
Did not like TANF	4.8%
Too much paperwork or hassle	4.3%
Obtained reliable transportation	3.7%
Got married	3.7%
Health improved	3.0%
Could not provide all the needed documentation	3.0%
Applied for TANF, application pending	3.0%
Youngest child turned 18 years of age	2.2%
Other	10.1%

Source: Statewide survey of families leaving TANF in July–
September 2000.
*It is interesting that in a sample that excluded households
that had reached their time limit, 6.6 percent of the families
believed they had.

fare office and meeting job expectations by being reliable, punctual, and present
at work.

Once at their jobs for a few months, virtually all TANF leavers lost their eligibility for TANF. However, even when they were employed, their finances remained precarious. As several women pointed out, receiving an employer's
paycheck did not mean they no longer needed assistance. In fact, when TANF
eligibility ended abruptly on the welfare office's notification of employment (or,
as was often the case, women were forced to pay back TANF and food stamp
overpayments when they delayed reporting), many women felt punished for
their entry into the workforce.

I've been penalized for working. They want you to get a job, but then they penalize you for that. It's much easier to get help when you're not working.

After a brief transitional period, women also lost some of the child care and Medicaid benefits associated with TANF. Others cited the welfare bureaucracies as too troublesome for the amount of money received. According to one respondent,

It's too big of a hassle, and I'm not going back. They made me go to the point where I don't want to go back. And if there's any way possible, I'm going to try to not go back.

Another respondent agreed:

Too much information is required in order to qualify. There's too much of a runaround.

What the Agency Records Showed

Agencies administering the TANF program were not always privy to the complex reasons families had for leaving TANF. However, we were able to use data from the administrative program files on TANF leavers to construct regression equations, a statistical technique that allowed us to calculate the importance of an individual factor or variable while holding all other variables constant. From this analysis, we determined that families were most likely to leave TANF if the mother was currently employed, if she "refused to register for employment services,"[3] or the family was one of the few two-parent families in which both parents were eligible for TANF (Table 6.3). Families with one of these characteristics were 5 to 10 percentage points more likely to leave TANF.[4]

These findings suggest that a number of families left TANF because their financial situation improved (through employment or the amount of child support received) or that they could share their work and parenting responsibilities with another adult (two-parent families). However, some features of the TANF program rules may have influenced families' decisions to leave TANF, such as the nature of the employment services for which some families "refused" to register and from which others were exempt, being subjected to TANF penalties, and participating in the Choices program when families used it beyond the assessment phase. The effects of program requirements appeared stronger during the second wave of data collection, after a number of program rules had been changed.

The influence of some of the factors on family life changed somewhat between the two time periods of our study. Most notably, current employment be-

Table 6.3. Major Factors Predicting Exit from TANF (Monthly Regressions Using Administrative Data)

Cohort 1 (April 1998–June 1999): Dependent mean = .16; N = 971,176
Cohort 2 (July–September 2000): Dependent mean = .16; N = 132,72

Variable description	Cohort 1	Cohort 2
Foster care placement made for any children in prior 3 months	.306	.464
Currently employed (any earnings; monthly estimate from quarterly earnings)	.099	.067
Two-parent family (TANF-UP)	.052	.057
Substantiated investigations of abuse or neglect for any children in prior 3 months	.048	.053
Caretaker refused to register for employment services	.044	.058
Percent of time employed (any earnings) in prior 24 months	.022	.025
Percent of time receiving TANF in prior 12 months	.016	−.032
Caretaker exempt from registration for employment services due to caring for child	.012	.034
Choices participation beyond assessment during current TANF spell	.006	.025
Percent of time receiving food stamps in prior 12 months	−.018	−.037
Caretaker race Black	−.022	−.028

Source: Regressions using administrative data for all TANF recipients from April 1998–June 1999 and July–September 2000.
Note: To be included in this table, variables had to be statistically significant in both time periods and had to increase or decrease the chances of exit by at least 2.5 percentage points. Complete regression results are included in Appendix B.

came a less important predictor of exit over time. For example, employed leavers in the first cohort were more likely by 10 percentage points to exit in any given month (.099 in Table 6.3), compared to an increase of only 7 percentage points (.067 in Table 6.3) for the second cohort. We attribute the findings for this variable in part to changes in the Earned Income Disregard policy that occurred between the two data collection periods. This policy allowed TANF recipients in the later period to retain more of their earnings before reaching the threshold of financial ineligibility for TANF. Thus, families were more likely to be able to stay on TANF for some period of employment.

Black respondents and those who received food stamps for longer time periods were more likely to remain on TANF. In statistical analyses, race and ethnicity sometimes misleadingly emerge as highly significant variables. Although race and ethnicity have a strong association with outcome variables, other statistically unaccounted-for variables that are strongly correlated with a certain racial or ethnic group may actually be producing these differences. As is sometimes the case, once variables such as the nature of employment are appropriately measured and accounted for, the association of race or ethnicity with the outcome is diminished and even disappears in later analyses.

Two other variables had strong influences in the regression models: the placement of children in foster care and substantiated cases of abuse or neglect. Both of these variables strongly correlated with families' departure from TANF. This relationship can be understood in the context of policies that automatically disqualify families from receiving benefits on behalf of children who are physically removed from the home. As a result, the relationship between Child Protective Services involvement and TANF disqualification is quite strong. Fortunately, circumstances related to child removal occurred in less than 2 percent of study families.

Getting a Job

Because employment was a primary way for TANF recipients to leave welfare and one of the explicit goals of welfare reform, we developed several analyses to determine why some TANF leavers were more successful in getting jobs than others. However, before discussing the results of these regression analyses, we should establish that families and researchers defined employment in different ways. The employment measures from administrative data sources (which are used in the regression analyses) were derived from quarterly earnings reports from the Unemployment Insurance (UI) system, which covers almost all formal employment in the state. So, when TANF leavers worked for employers who reported their incomes to the UI system, their earnings for that period became part of the administrative data we used. Although several definitions (in terms of number of months worked, amount of earnings, or other factors) can be constructed from this widely used research data source, none of them would substantially change the results we discuss here. Regardless of the definition, between 48 and 55 percent of all TANF leavers were employed in the first calendar quarter after their families left welfare.

Another definition of employment—the self-perception of employment—emerged in the statewide survey and the qualitative interviews with TANF leavers. In both surveys and interviews, many former TANF recipients described themselves as employed, even though they were not currently earning any income. Conversely, some reported informal or agricultural employment that was not captured through the UI wage system. Thus, each data source is associated with some degree of error in terms of either overreporting or underreporting employment. Even so, the absolute share of families who left TANF for employment was roughly 50 percent of all families in the study. More important for our discussion here, the factors associated with whether or not someone got a job seem unaffected by the precise definition of employment.

We determined associations with employment using two different types of regression models, both of which allowed us to assess the strength of the relationship between an individual variable and employment while holding all other variables constant.[5] In Model 1, we used only data from the administrative data sources. In this analysis, we tracked families who left TANF from April 1998 through June 1999 (Cohort 1) for each of the following eighteen months, and families who left TANF from June through September 2000 (Cohort 2) for each of the following six months. In Model 2, we combined administrative data with data from the statewide survey to determine which factors were associated with employment for families who left TANF from July through September 2000.

Each of these approaches had its advantages and disadvantages. The administrative data regression model was based on a much larger sample that used the entire population of all TANF leavers in Texas, producing more stable estimates than the smaller sample used for the second set of combined regressions. Also, because the administrative data tracked quarterly employment over time, there were more frequent data points, which better accounted for changes in family status than the combined data set, which measured only employment sometime within one three-month period. Conversely, the combined regressions with both survey and administrative data included variables that could not be located in administrative data (such as health status, transportation needs and problems, and child care outside the subsidized system) yet seemed to be important factors in families' ability to get and retain employment.[6]

Variables Positively Associated with Employment

In both models, the strongest association with current employment was the length of time a person had been employed during the prior two years. Adults who had been employed for the entire two-year period before leaving TANF increased their rates of current employment by 57 percentage points over those not employed during that interval. Although the relationship of prior employment to current employment may seem intuitively obvious, it supports the contention that helping to maintain TANF recipients' continuous work efforts until they are stable should increase their long-term employability.

In addition to prior employment, a number of other conditions also improved the likelihood of employment for TANF leavers, although the configuration of these conditions varied depending on whether we used only administrative data in our regressions (Model 1) or both administrative and survey data sources (Model 2). These conditions included the following:

- *Use of child care outside a child's home,* as measured by the use of subsidized child care after leaving TANF in both models[7] and the youngest child cared for by a nonrelative in that person's home (Model 2).

- *Activities that connected TANF families with the labor market,* as measured by participation in the Choices program in the most recent period on TANF (Model 1), having looked for a job in the past six months (Model 2), or participation in non-Choices employment services while on TANF (Model 2).

- *Having or needing access to medical care for children after leaving TANF,* as measured by receipt of children's Medicaid after leaving TANF (both models) and children needing medical care but not being able to afford the doctor's visit (Model 2).

- *Having reliable transportation,* as measured by the absence of transportation problems that interfered with employment (Model 2).

The relative importance of these variables within each of the regression models is shown in Table 6.4. The association of race and ethnicity with employment diminishes when key variables related to access to and use of services, among other factors, are included in the combined data regression model. In Model 1, which used only the more limited variables available through the administrative data, Black and Hispanic adults appear significantly more likely to become employed than white adults. However, once additional family variables available from the survey (such as family structure, type of child care used, and access to medical care) are added to the Model 2 regressions, race and ethnicity are no longer predictive factors of either employment or return to TANF.

Model 2 provides strong evidence that families that were able to access the supportive services (Choices, transitional Medicaid, transitional child care) designed to help them find employment were fairly successful. Overall, our findings highlight the role that noncash benefits for low-income families (child care, medical insurance, and transportation) played in helping TANF families find employment (see Bloom et al., 2005, for a discussion of program supports).

Table 6.4. Major Factors Predicting Employment

Model 1: Monthly Regressions Using Statewide Universe of Administrative Data

Cohort 1 (April 1998–June 1999): Dependent mean = .56; N = 1,777,878
Cohort 2 (July–September 2000): Dependent mean = .56; N = 132,211

Variable description	Cohort 1	Cohort 2
Percent of time employed (any earnings) in prior 24 months	.572	.579
Any subsidized child care receipt during off-TANF spell	.130	.085
Choices participation beyond assessment during prior TANF spell	.092	.123
Medicaid receipt for any children during off-TANF spell	.088	.065
Caretaker race Black	.064	.028
Caretaker race Hispanic	.047	.041
Any Medicaid receipt during off-TANF spell	.040	.030
Two-parent family (TANF-UP)	−.072	−.048

Source: Regression analysis using administrative data for all TANF leavers April 1998–June 1999 and July–September 2000.
Note: To be included in this table, variables had to be statistically significant in both time periods and had to increase or decrease chances of exit by at least 2.5 percentage points. Complete regression results are included in Appendix B.

Variables Negatively Associated with Employment

Model 1 identifies being a caretaker in a two-parent family as the factor having the strongest negative association with TANF leavers' employment rates. This implies a family structure in which one parent worked while the other cared for the children and was not employed. The caretaker was then less likely to be employed. Although a number of other variables were statistically related to lower rates of employment, none was very strong. In light of the high rates of serious medical issues in the survey data, one parent's health problems might have made it difficult for that parent to hold a job, but this was not reflected in the regression results.

By including the family survey variables in the Model 2 regressions, we were able to achieve a more satisfying explanation of what may be behind the reduced rates of employment for some TANF leavers. Former TANF recipients who were not employed after leaving TANF, a group that has been overlooked in much of the welfare research, made up about 45 percent of our sample. The additional

Table 6.4. Major Factors Predicting Employment

Model 2: Point-in-Time Regressions for Random Sample of Leavers

Survey sample, administrative data only: Dependent mean = .57; N = 682
Administrative data plus survey data: Dependent mean = .57; N = 678

Variable description	Administrative variables only	Administrative plus survey variables
As of last month on TANF, percent of time employed (any earnings) in prior 24 months	.596	.515
Any subsidized child care receipt during off-TANF spell	.229	.240
Non-Choices employment services received during prior TANF spell	.140	.105
Medicaid receipt for any children during off-TANF spell	.131	.129
Youngest child cared for by babysitter or other nonrelative at that person's home		.117
Children needed to see a doctor but couldn't afford to		.100
Looked for work in past 6 months		.090
Reliability of usual transportation		.090
Experienced barriers to employment in two or more areas (child care, health, transportation)		−.092
Care for youngest child myself		−.123
Married and living with spouse		−.124
Exited TANF because of child support receipt		−.133
Returned to TANF because of divorce or separation		−.171
Exited TANF because could not provide necessary documentation		−.227
Widowed		−.270

Source: Regression analysis using administrative and survey data for families leaving TANF in July–September 2000.
Note: To be included in this table, variables had to increase or decrease probability of employment by at least 8 percentage points. Complete regression results are included in Appendix B.

survey variables greatly enhanced our understanding of this large and under-investigated subpopulation of welfare recipients.

The Model 2 regressions establish that some former TANF caretakers were reliant on the earnings or child support in the form of contributions through earned wages of their spouses, former spouses, or fathers of their children. The data show that being widowed, having received TANF because of divorce or separation, having exited TANF due to receiving child support, or being married and living with a spouse (combined data)[8] are factors related to a decrease in the likelihood of being employed. As illustrated by the family stories recounted in earlier chapters, difficulties with child care, particularly parents' need to care for a youngest child themselves, were related to a decreased chance of employment. The existence of at least two barriers to employment in the areas of child care, food, housing, or transportation was also negatively related to employment. The variable "experienced multiple barriers to employment" lowered employment rates by an additional 9 percentage points beyond the effects of each individual barrier included in this measure.

Finally, the small share of adults who reported difficulty meeting the require-ments of the welfare program (such as inability to provide the necessary docu-mentation) also were less likely to be employed. Although this condition was strongly associated with lower levels of employment, only 3 percent of surveyed leavers fell into this category. So it is likely that even though quite a few families mentioned these factors as reasons for leaving TANF, all but a few families were still able to get jobs.

Why Some Families Returned to TANF

A large number of the families left TANF only to return to welfare within a rela-tively short period. To get a better picture of why so many families were unable to sustain themselves in the long term without TANF, we analyzed why short-term leavers (those families who returned to TANF within six months) needed TANF. As in our explorations of the reasons why families left TANF, we used both quantitative and descriptive, qualitative data to answer this question. Again, we used our survey responses from families who returned to TANF, as well as the re-gression equations, which drew on the administrative data available. In these re-gression analyses we combined information from both administrative and sur-vey data sources into one set of equations. This analysis focuses on those families who returned to TANF within six months after leaving, so it is extremely helpful in explaining why short-term leavers had such difficulty surviving without cash welfare assistance.

Table 6.5. Reasons for Returning to TANF, Cohort 2

If you are now receiving TANF: Why did you go back on TANF?
(✓ all that apply):

Total number of respondents: 155

Lost job/laid off job/stopped working	41.3%
Needed Medicaid for self or children	36.1%
Lost housing	20.7%
Income dropped	18.7%
Lost transportation/car broke down	16.8%
Became pregnant/just gave birth	14.8%
Became ill	14.8%
Divorce/separation	12.3%
Lost child support/stopped receiving child support	12.3%
Needed to care for another household member	11.6%
Lost child care	11.6%
Other	29.0%

Source: Statewide survey of families leaving TANF in July–September 2000.

What Families Told Us

Families who had returned to TANF were asked to explain the circumstances of their return. Because the survey allowed respondents to cite multiple reasons for returning to TANF, families often listed more than one. Forty-one percent of the respondents who returned to TANF did so at least in part because they had lost a job. However, nearly as many (36 percent) said that they returned at least in part to requalify for needed Medicaid benefits either for themselves or for their children. Survey respondents had numerous reasons for going back on welfare (Table 6.5). Their complicated life stories showed that families were often experiencing more than one of these factors at a time.

What the Regression Equations Revealed

Although the survey encouraged families to elaborate the multiple reasons for their TANF return, organizations that set policies usually want to understand which of the items that families mentioned were the key reasons associated with their returns to TANF. We were able to establish this by using a regression model that combined administrative and survey data to suggest why some families

Table 6.6. Major Factors Predicting TANF Reentry
Point-in-Time Regressions for Random Sample of Leavers

Survey sample, administrative data only: Dependent mean = .24; N = 681;
Administrative data plus survey data: Dependent mean = .24; N = 677

Variable description	Administrative variables only	Administrative plus survey variables
As of last month on TANF, percent of time employed (any earnings) in prior 24 months	.227	.225
As of last month on TANF, percent of time receiving food stamps in prior 12 months	.167	.118
Any subsidized child care received during prior TANF spell	.078	.083
Caretaker refused to register for employment services	−.087	−.131
Caretaker education and work history indicate serious impediments to employment (tier 3)	−.096	−.087
Any food stamps receipt during off-TANF spell	−.131	−.109
Received assistance with fuel costs in past 6 months		.339
Youngest child cared for by babysitter or other non-relative at that person's home		.138
Received any assistance with housing costs in past 6 months		.113
Own or share a car or truck		−.095
Needed to see a doctor but couldn't afford to		−.134
Exited TANF because another adult contributed money		−.152
Exited TANF because obtained reliable transportation		−.160
Received assistance with telephone costs in past 6 months		−.183
Any income from Unemployment Insurance last month		−.198
Exited TANF because got married		−.233
Widowed		−.248
Currently employed		−.252

Source: Regression analysis using administrative and survey data for families leaving TANF in July–September 2000.
Note: To be included in this table, variables had to increase or decrease probability of TANF reentry by at least 8 percentage points. Complete regression results are included in Appendix B.

were successful in staying off TANF while others were not. This analysis showed us that caretakers were less likely to return to TANF when they were currently employed, earned higher wages at TANF exit, received financial contributions from another source (another adult, Social Security benefits for widows, or UI payments, for instance), left TANF because of marriage, had stable transportation, or needed money for medical care (Table 6.6).

Conversely, respondents with a history of prior employment (but not necessarily current employment) were more likely to return to TANF, suggesting again that job loss often contributed to a family's return to TANF. This finding also implies that the employment of some TANF leavers was not very stable. In addition to losing a job, those families who needed assistance with food or housing costs, received child care through the Choices program while on TANF, or had their youngest child cared for by a nonrelative were also more likely to return to TANF.

It is interesting to note that, although families often mentioned needing Medicaid as one reason why they returned to TANF, the variables that measured the receipt of these services were not significant in the regression equations. Thus, although the need for Medicaid may have seemed important to those families that returned to TANF, it did not emerge in the formal analysis as a key difference explaining why some families returned to TANF and other, similarly situated families did not. Instead, families who cited needing more money for medical care were less likely to return to TANF as a strategy for obtaining that care. Another possible explanation may be related to the meaning of the Medicaid variable. We measured whether adults and children enrolled in Medicaid, not whether they actually used it (a situation similar to having health insurance but not filing a claim).[9]

Implications of the Analysis

This analysis clearly illustrates families' utilization of multiple strategies for obtaining the resources needed to stay off welfare. Some families used a combination of employment and supportive services to enable them to stay off the rolls. They appeared able to do this more successfully if they earned more money and were connected with other services that provided additional economic supports (such as subsidized child care and some type of medical insurance coverage) that facilitated employment for many mothers. Other families relied on earnings and income from other family members to stay off welfare (these resources were either in combination with their own earnings or in lieu of working themselves). These families also tended to be more successful in staying off welfare.

The group most at risk of returning to TANF within the first six months, however, seemed to be a subset of families who left TANF for employment that was not stable. These families also seemed to lack the level of external supports exhibited by the two groups of families discussed above. Although the subsidized child care they received while on TANF increased their chances of finding a job, it was also related to a greater likelihood of returning to welfare, perhaps because of losing access to child care when they lost a job. Other factors associated with higher returns to TANF, such as needing help with food or housing or having a child cared for by nonrelatives, suggest that this group of TANF leavers had a much weaker support network than other TANF leavers. Although some TANF leavers could draw on a range of supports, allowing them to ride out the challenges they encountered after leaving TANF, the group likely to return to TANF had fewer such supports in reserve.

We do not want to leave the impression that many families were able to leave poverty. Although we were not able to capture poverty measures as we would have liked, we do know that most families in this study, based on their earned wages and their eligibility for services, were poor throughout the time we followed them. Among these low-income families, though, some families were able to accrue resources through their social and economic networks that allowed them to maintain or improve their families' well-being. Families that stayed off TANF were also more likely to be healthy as well. However, almost all families were in poverty throughout the period of the study. Furthermore, changes in circumstances, such as the onset of ill health or the loss of informal resources, could make families significantly more vulnerable to a return to TANF.

SEVEN

Low-Income Families and TANF Policies

What Works and What Doesn't

·

MOST LOW-INCOME FAMILIES in low-wage jobs strived for as much financial independence as they could manage, even during periods of welfare dependence. About half the families that left welfare did so when someone in the family got a job. However, families also left welfare for other reasons: they were unsuccessful in managing the TANF application and recertification process, or a parent got married or began receiving child support, or someone in the family became eligible for Supplemental Security Income (SSI). Whether working or not, most families remained impoverished after their departure from welfare and were still at risk of returning to welfare.

In this book, we've explored how families experienced the departure from welfare and how they tried to make a living afterward. Our study included families who left TANF because they got jobs, became ineligible because of other income they received, or were unable or unwilling to meet all the requirements to continue receiving welfare. At the time of our study, welfare reform was sufficiently new that families had not yet reached their state time limits. By design, the few families that had met the state's time limits were excluded from our sample. Therefore, in some ways, we might expect the families studied here to be a little better off than the welfare leavers to come in later years, because none of these families had been forced off welfare by time limits. Furthermore, in this sample, the entire family had left TANF: not just the adults but the children too were no longer on welfare.

Although the welfare rolls declined substantially following welfare reform, and poverty rates among the overall Texas population declined in the late 1990s, the large majority of families who left TANF during this period remained in poverty not just while on welfare but also during its aftermath. Indeed, less than 5 percent of the families leaving TANF moved out of poverty in the eighteen months after their departure. They joined the ranks of the working poor. Many were impoverished single parents, others were part of the state's unusually large population of impoverished two-parent families.

Thus, what we found was a policy that moved people off welfare very effectively but did little to alleviate poverty. The welfare rolls fell rapidly during the post–welfare reform years. Far fewer Texas families used TANF than had used Aid to Families with Dependent Children (AFDC) in the pre–welfare reform period, some because of increased employment and other economic supports but others because the welfare rules were onerous or confusing to them. However, once off welfare, families remained in poverty, many without consistent and adequate health insurance (particularly for low-income adults), child care, and training and job support services. Unfortunately, their lives did not seem particularly different than when they were on welfare, nor did their lives seem different from those of welfare leavers prior to welfare reform. Welfare reform led to few long-term changes in the lives of the low-income families we met.

Except for those families who left TANF as a consequence of welfare reform requirements, reasons for exits from and returns to welfare have not changed, nor have the factors influencing the success or failure of welfare exits. Families left welfare when they got a job or family resources changed (a parent married or gained child support, a child reached eighteen years of age, or family members found they could provide extra support), and they and their family members were healthy enough to forgo welfare-related health benefits. They returned to welfare when a parent lost a job, a partner left or child support stopped, family members could no longer help, or health problems complicated their lives.

Just as the experiences of TANF leavers resembled the experiences of AFDC leavers, the experiences of Texas TANF leavers in the post–welfare reform era resembled TANF leavers from other states in their use of government benefits, employment, and earnings. However, Texas families were different in that they were somewhat more likely to return to TANF than those in other states. We might attribute this difference to either the relatively lower post–TANF economic supports, or the less restrictive Texas time limits and diversion policies in effect during the time of this study, or the fact that Texas welfare recipients have historically tended to cycle between welfare and work.

We were able to view the lives of nonemployed TANF leavers more clearly from the current study than was possible from the pre–welfare reform studies that used only administrative data. By combining data sources and analytic techniques, we closely investigated the ways in which family outcomes were related to different welfare policies, as well as the ways in which families experienced these welfare policies. This approach allows us to better understand why certain policies led to improved outcomes for families while other policies left families vulnerable to less sustained periods of employment, increased hardship, and more frequent returns to the welfare system.

In this chapter, we discuss the nature of welfare policies that seemed to improve family outcomes as well as those that seemed to pose difficulties for the family. We explore the nature of the jobs post-welfare families were likely to acquire and the possibilities and difficulties these jobs introduced in their lives. We conclude by providing an overview of the larger policy directions that could benefit low-wage families, especially those who, like the families we studied for this book, have recently left welfare and are trying to survive in the post–welfare reform world.

The Value of Welfare Policies

Individual welfare policies and program guidelines were evaluated differently by recipients. Some TANF and related policies improved families' employment possibilities and overall economic well-being. Other policies, however, created confusion and additional challenges for families struggling to balance work and family responsibilities. In general, subsidized child care, transitional Medicaid benefits, and Choices (job search and placement) services seemed to increase families' income and the likelihood of being employed. Furthermore, recipients themselves emphasized the importance and value these supports had for their families. However, because these programs were not fully funded, and program guidelines prioritized families currently receiving TANF and very recent TANF leavers, many former TANF families were left without access to key resources that might have reduced the likelihood that they would return to TANF. Though eligible for services, most TANF leavers did not receive subsidized child care vouchers. Most, particularly adults, eventually lost their Medicaid benefits, as well as their access to workforce development services. Since this research was conducted, Texas has continued to provide low levels of cash benefits for TANF recipients. In keeping with its limited investment in the development of welfare recipients' human capital, it has maintained its focus on putting people in jobs quickly, with far fewer resources devoted to recipients' education and training.

Furthermore, since the time of our study, the rules in Texas have increased in severity in a number of ways. Exemptions for parents with young children were lowered again, from age two to one. Texas also introduced harsher penalties for violations of the personal responsibility agreement. For example, full family sanctions, or removal of the entire family from welfare benefits (rather than just the adult parent), might be applied to families who failed to meet requirements. Participation in Choices, which offers some job assistance services but also starts the clock for state time limits, became a mandatory requirement in all Texas counties and was eventually enforced even in rural counties, where there is little program infrastructure and where high local unemployment rates make a successful job hunt unlikely. The state also engaged in an unsuccessful legal battle to cut the Medicaid benefits of families who had not maintained children's regular health care and inoculation schedules. The Children's Health Insurance Program (CHIP), a program intended to increase health insurance coverage for children of the working poor, was introduced just after the period of our data collection, only to suffer major funding cuts in 2003, which resulted in thousands of children losing their health insurance. As a result, the overall service environment became harsher for TANF leavers than it was during the time of our study.

On the other hand, there have been some efforts to ease the confusion surrounding eligibility and benefits. For instance, Texas is in the process of instituting call centers where people may establish eligibility without an office appointment.

The Labor Force Experience

A large proportion of Texas TANF families have always tried to get jobs. Unfortunately, stricter time limits and sanction policies did not improve these families' chances of finding stable and sustainable employment. Some families who faced losing TANF were still unable to locate work, particularly in regions with high unemployment. Without TANF or a paid job, they were likely to fall into deeper poverty. As welfare policies continue to be recast, more careful consideration is necessary to determine whether the employment barriers families experience are specific to the individual family or to the larger economic environment in which they live. Policy-makers should also take into account what services families need to remain stable while working in low-wage jobs with few benefits.

Even urban families that find work may also find that their low-wage, low-skill jobs cannot meet the needs of their households. The earnings from a full-time minimum-wage job would not raise a family with children out of poverty (Schexnayder et al., 2006). Families who do sustain such employment and lose transitional child care and Medicaid benefits are vulnerable to any number of destabilizing events or crises. These families may also find themselves incurring large amounts of debt over time. Current Texas welfare policies encourage families to get jobs and leave welfare quickly yet fail to support them as new workers. It is likely that policies that extended former recipients' transitional benefits for a longer time period or provided additional services not accessible through low wage jobs would facilitate more successful and stable entries into the labor force. Current policies increase the likelihood that families with only limited social support will slide back onto the welfare rolls. We do not yet know what will happen to these most fragile families once they exceed their time limits and the TANF program becomes closed to them.

The Larger Policy Arena and Low-Income Families:
Lessons from the Texas Experience

The Texas welfare experience represents one possible direction of welfare policy across the nation as the population and the economy continue to change in ways we described in Chapter 2. Changes in Texas were characterized by a high number of working-age adults entering the labor force with low educational levels. They and their families confronted an economy in which sustainable wages were often reserved for those workers who had either more marketable skills or more education. Although the need for state investment in education, training, and workforce supports (such as child care and medical insurance) increased, Texas, along with many other states, faced budgetary shortfalls that curtailed expenditures in these areas. Even as states reduced their spending on such programs, the federal government, rather than filling in the gaps, was also moving in the direction of cutting rather than expanding its poverty programs. Even with an economic recovery in the past several years, more families have been slipping below the poverty line. Even so, the reauthorization of TANF (in January 2006), combined with the 2006 budget enacted by Congress, cut funds for Medicaid and child-support enforcement and increased TANF work requirements without allocating sufficient child care funds to support this policy change (U.S. House of Representatives, 2006).

The survey and interviews we conducted identified three primary components to families' stability: having at least a modest and dependable income, having health insurance for both children and parents, and having affordable and reliable child care. Our families' experiences suggest ways in which policies could strengthen family life in each of these areas. With the exception of Medicaid receipt, our regression analyses verified that the same policies that families valued also improved their chances of becoming employed.

Program Regulations

Overall, our analysis suggests that the ways in which Texas welfare programs have been regulated undermines the long-term self-sufficiency of some low-income families. Complex rules and requirements for proving program eligibility interfered with welfare recipients' functioning as responsible and responsive employees. From 1995 through 2000, frequent changes in TANF criteria led to confusion among both recipients and agency staff members as to service eligibility and requirements. Both the statistical and qualitative analyses identified policies that hampered families' efforts to both work and care for their families. In particular, navigating the TANF program's bureaucracies of elaborate paperwork, complex eligibility and recertification criteria, and the various aspects of the personal responsibility agreement was extremely difficult. Families also reported specific barriers associated with unexpectedly encountering eligibility restrictions regarding family members who were cosigners for car loans, as well as a lack of supports and options for those recipients facing transportation and other employment barriers.

Families' confusion about TANF regulations seemed at least a partial reflection of the lack of clarity many caseworkers had about program policies. Furthermore, the eligibility criteria and recertification requirements for non-TANF programs were demanding for families in terms of their time and energy. The Food Stamps Employment and Training program, which included work requirements for families with children more than five years old, left many food stamp applicants confused about whether they had qualified for benefits. Understanding Medicaid eligibility was similarly difficult. Medicaid eligibility was determined according to several factors, including the age of the child, family size, and the family's income. Even CHIP, a program for low-income families ineligible for Medicaid, underwent a number of changes that resulted in fewer eligible children across the state. In fact, a substantial number of children were dropped from the CHIP program within a few years of enrolling. Because eligibility criteria for these programs changed over time, families' understanding of the ways that programs functioned quickly became out-of-date, leaving families unsure of what they actually knew.

Not every policy change adopted during this time period had a negative impact on families. For instance, the increase in the Earned Income Disregard, which allowed low-income families to omit or disregard most of their earnings before being considered financially ineligible for welfare, allowed families to keep their TANF benefits for a few months after the recipient had started working.

However, overall policies for low-income families gave priority to those on TANF or in the process of transitioning off TANF over the working poor (including the two-parent impoverished families, who made up half of this group). Working poor families remained vulnerable in terms of what should really matter to society: sufficient stability to raise their children in a healthy and secure environment. While experiencing low and often irregular earnings, these families were more likely to live without health care, without subsidized child care (in the event they needed it), and without access to even the small cash transfer offered by TANF. With only the low wages offered by available jobs and limited access to benefits, our current policy environment leaves these families with minimal resources to keep their children healthy and to allow parents to take advantage of educational and training opportunities that would improve their own lifelong job prospects. The demographic trends in Texas suggest that an investment in such families is necessary to sustain a healthy labor force and growing economy.

As for the country as a whole, it is important to keep in mind the enormous variation in the composition of the different regions of Texas when developing policies that affect families throughout the state. Policies developed for primarily urban areas, for example, do not necessarily serve the needs of more rural families. Texas currently gives families vouchers for subsidized child care and enrolls them in Medicaid, but families living in rural areas may not benefit from these programs if such services are scarce in the communities where they live. In rural areas, child care is sometimes in short supply, and providers may not be enrolled in the subsidy system. Health care may be available only at a considerable distance, and some providers, particularly in underserved rural areas, may turn away new patients and Medicaid patients. Increasing our sensitivity to the differences that exist among families and across the environments where they work and raise children would allow us to better target programs to meet individual families' needs.

Texas has begun piloting a somewhat controversial phone call-in system to determine eligibility for most human services programs. Rural residents might find such a system more accessible than the current approach of traveling great distances to apply for services. Such an approach, if well-designed and implemented, might also make it easier for families to convey information without having to take off time from work to wait in welfare offices. Parents already juggling child care and new jobs often experience mandatory appointments at the welfare office as a risk to their jobs. Families may appreciate the ability to conduct their appointments by telephone, particularly in an already restricted system that gives relatively few families access to real case management services. However, this pilot program has caused considerable controversy in the policy community. Such a system could eliminate both initial case management services and special considerations for recipients with unusual or extenuating circumstances. In addition, families who have received assistance from case managers who approach family services in more holistic manner highly value their case management and report that they are better able to get and keep a job because of the support they receive. The contractor hired to run this new call-center-based eligibility determination system also had major implementation problems, resulting in many applications being erroneously rejected. As of this writing, HHSC has suspended further rollout of the call-center system and resumed its old eligibility determination procedures while the contractor works on resolving its startup problems. The future fate of this initiative is unclear (Texas Health and Human Services Commission, 2006).

Jobs, Income, and Employment Supports

Texas is one of many states that have experimented with welfare reform. Some of these experiments have identified promising policy initiatives that increase welfare leavers' chances of finding and keeping jobs. Such policies allow workers to combine wages with other sources of income, stabilize their families, and eventually move out of poverty. Given the relatively short timeline for TANF recipients to stabilize themselves once they find work, they require jobs that pay above-poverty wages and also provide access to core services, such as health insurance and child care. Other research has confirmed that the jobs held by TANF leavers typically do not provide such supports (Loprest, 2003; Zedlewski, 2002). Therefore, successful and promising policy options include increasing the minimum wage, providing employers incentives to offer certain benefits, changing the tax code (such as the Earned Income Tax Credit) so that working families can retain more income, and adjusting welfare programs to enable long-term employment. From a policy perspective, we recommend a four-pronged approach to address this complex set of problems.

First, we must develop strategies that increase the take-home pay of workers and allow them the workplace flexibility to balance their responsibilities as parents as well as employees. Although some states have piloted programs that offer direct wage supplements for welfare recipients working in low-wage jobs, more systemic approaches may more effectively provide the necessary income for families to achieve a modest sense of economic stability and well-being. Higher earnings allow families to better provide for their families, as well as become more stable in their employment. With more dependable income, families are also able to acquire the transportation and other resources that allow them to be more dependable employees.

Second, benefits such as health insurance, paid sick days, and paid holidays allow families to better meet both job and family responsibilities. However, few of the jobs occupied by TANF leavers provide such benefits. Furthermore, after the first few months off TANF, TANF leavers are increasingly unlikely to have access to public benefits to supplement those provided by their jobs.

TANF regulations that require mothers to work a fixed number of hours do not take into account the nature of the jobs that women typically get as they depart TANF. Retail and service jobs, which are among those most available to TANF recipients, are likely to have variable and rotating hours from week to week and even from day to day. Mothers who work variable hours may be able to comply with program requirements one week but not the next, depending on the schedule their employer assigns to them.

Alternatively, we can respond with policies that provide impoverished families with supports and encourage their employers to adopt more expansive employee benefit policies. Extending transitional health insurance and child care beyond the currently brief transitional period would allow families leaving TANF more time to acquire either the income or employee benefits needed to deal with typical work-family challenges, such as the onset of illness or changes in child care arrangements.

Third, we should review existing tax laws to ensure that they provide a progressive income ladder for working families. We must also improve our techniques for educating low-income families about existing tax laws that might enhance their families' income. Although this study was unable to properly assess families' use of the EITC, federal estimates suggest that expansion of this tax benefit in the late 1990s lifted 4.7 million people (including 2.6 million children) out of poverty in 1999. Although the General Accounting Office estimates that 86 percent of eligible households claim this deduction, welfare leavers seem far less likely to take advantage of this tax benefit. This underutilization may occur either because families are unaware of the benefit (Cauthen, 2002) or because they are unable to use it, since they are not filing tax returns.

Broader policies could support TANF leavers, the working poor, and the growing group of the middle class (Angel et al., 2006) that is struggling with issues such as contract work and access to health insurance. Increases in the minimum wage or living wage policies could lead more families to economic self-sufficiency. Universal health insurance would not leave families uninsured when families are ineligible for means-tested insurance but have no access to employer-assisted insurance. A more universal and coordinated child care system would alleviate the pressures of child care costs on families in low-wage employment.

Finally, our policies should reflect the reality that some families may need extended support beyond that permitted by current time limits. Some families are heavily burdened by the illness or chronic medical condition of a family member. Others live in areas with scarce to nonexistent employment opportunities. Some families need long-term assistance with housing. Some families need more education and training before they can compete for jobs that provide dependable and sustainable income. In the long run, more stringent welfare policies can only work when coupled with supportive policies for those families who lack the personal resources and social networks to make it on their own in the short term.

Recognizing the barriers these welfare leavers will face in the labor market, some states have combined tighter limits on welfare with extended access to training and education. These states have also extended the time period in which families can combine welfare and work. Texas' implementation of Work First reflected the stringency of its financial eligibility requirements for TANF; as a result, TANF recipients were quickly moved off welfare and into first jobs. Once employed adults left TANF, they also lost access to many of the programs that could have helped them get additional training while employed in their new jobs. As our data demonstrate, we need strategies to help families increase their long-term earning potential, while they can continue to receive enough short-term support to stabilize their families. Without such strategies in place, many families are unlikely to earn enough to support their families in the long term.

We also need to develop strategies that draw assistance from fathers. Such policies can include improved efforts to collect and distribute child support payments. However, father financial contributions can also be improved through an investment in education and training for which fathers are eligible and which in turn give them access to better-paid jobs (Looney and Schexnayder, 2004; Schroeder et al., 2004).

Policy Recommendations

Based on our glimpse into the lives of the many Texas families trying to leave TANF and establish a better life, we offer the following recommendations to improve the economic well-being of our poorest citizens:

1. Redesign services so that low-income families have sufficient time to participate in the workforce and simultaneously be good parents to their children.
   a. Adopt simple program rules that don't discourage work or make it impossible to adhere to those rules without missing work.
   b. Eliminate disincentives for independence.

2. Reconceptualize and destigmatize welfare benefits by viewing them as another form of unemployment insurance, but one with a broader funding base than only employers' contributions. We need to accept the reality that families may need to move between work and welfare as they go through difficult times and adjust to changes in the labor force.

3. Adopt a consumer education approach to inform potential eligible families about services available to help them obtain and keep jobs. We need to differentiate between those services that foster continued dependence from those that contribute to independence. After differentiating among these services, we should fully fund programs of the latter type and develop a sensible approach for families who need fewer external supports as their personal resources improve.

4. Deliver services in a manner that does not make unwarranted distinctions among types of families (such as single-parent and two-parent, TANF and working poor), while developing services more tailored to families who live in geographic areas with differing levels of infrastructure and access to employment.

5. Adopt more efficient and innovative methods of service delivery (such as determining eligibility by telephone) while maintaining access to the types of case management services that some families need and that can best be provided face-to-face.

6. Recognize that in the current economy, many hardworking, employed, low-income families will not have jobs with regular, full-time hours. We can use both social supports and tax laws to increase their income levels and thereby improve their chances of staying employed while adequately supporting their families.

7. Invest in the future earning potential of low-income families by providing them with more education and training options and creating opportunities for families to combine work and social supports.

8. Consider increases in the minimum wage or living wage legislation to bring the earnings of low-wage workers above the poverty line and ap-

proaching economic self-sufficiency. Provide more universal access to health insurance and child care.

9. Develop programs to support and improve the earnings of children's noncustodial parents, and improve the child support collection system.

Revamping our policies to support, rather than punish, young parents, both mothers and fathers, as they make the transition into their adult lives as workers and parents would be a sound investment in the future well-being of Texas families and the general economy. The parents who are heading a majority of the welfare families in Texas aspire to leave the cash assistance rolls, and most are able to achieve self-sufficiency by the time their children are old enough for high school. But sometimes these young adults rely on their own parents or extended family members to provide the financial support that would ease their transition from adolescence to adulthood. In addition, these young parents find themselves too preoccupied with the daily struggles of trying to work, pay bills, and raise young children to pursue the education and training needed to improve their workforce earning potential. As the demographics indicate, the stakes are quite high. If policy-makers fail to interrupt the dynamic created by our limited and punitive policies for impoverished families with young children, these children will grow up in impoverished families only to face the same challenges their parents faced, both on and off the welfare rolls.

Research Methods

This appendix reviews the multiple research methods that we used in the project on which this book is based (see Schexnayder, Lein, et al., 2002, for a more detailed discussion of the methodology). We also present the basic demographic analysis that was used to check the research populations and samples against each other. The research project combined (1) monitoring or descriptive research methods, (2) qualitative methods, and (3) econometric methods to study the lives of Texas families after welfare. The methods used for each population and time period are summarized in Table A.1 and described briefly. The table also shows the geographic coverage for each of these methods.

Monitoring and Descriptive Approaches

Monitoring and descriptive research approaches allow researchers to track certain populations over time or to summarize statistical information about them at various points in time. This study used two descriptive approaches: demographic and longitudinal analyses of TANF leavers using individual-level administrative program data maintained by various Texas state agencies, and a telephone and mail survey of a random statewide sample of TANF leavers (statewide survey) conducted approximately six months after the respondents left TANF.

Demographic and Longitudinal Analyses

A number of individual-level administrative data files from programs that serve Texas low-income families were linked to determine the demographic characteristics of families within each cohort and to follow families' program participation and economic well-being over time. The statewide universe of each cohort being studied is included in this analysis.

Data for this analysis included:

- The Texas Department of Human Services (DHS) SAVERR data system, which incorporated the following sources: TANF, food stamp, and Medicaid client strip tapes, which served as monthly snapshots of the case and client loads of these

Table A.1. Summary of Research Approaches and Time Periods Used

Time Period of Cohort Exit	Research Approaches / Data Sources Used	Geographic Coverage
April 1998–June 1999 (Cohort 1)	1. Descriptive analysis using administrative data 2 years prior through 18 months after event	Statewide universe
	2. Qualitative analysis using intensive interviews occurring sometime in the 15 months after event	Sub-state sample
	3. Econometric analysis using administrative data only	Statewide universe
July–September 2000 (Cohort 2)	1. Descriptive analyses	
	a. Administrative data 2 years prior through 6 months after exit	Statewide universe
	b. Telephone-mail survey within 6 months after exit	Statewide sample
	2. Econometric analysis	
	a. Administrative data only	Statewide universe
	b. Combination of administrative and survey data	Statewide sample

programs; cumulative warrant files containing historical records of actual cash assistance paid to cases, whether by check or by electronic benefits transfer; transaction files describing the disposition of TANF applications and recertifications, as well as other case changes; and Texas Works files, containing information completed by everyone entering a DHS office with the intent of applying for benefits to aid in the support of children.

- Texas Workforce Commission (TWC) data, which included reported employee wages by employer by calendar quarter; child care case and individual-level data, including spells of subsidized child care receipt, number of children receiving subsidized child care, and costs of subsidized care; Choices participation data, including monthly tallies of actual hours of participation; and participation in other workforce programs sponsored by TWC.

- Data from the Texas Office of the Attorney General, which included amounts of support paid by noncustodial parents monthly and the share that is disbursed to the state and to the custodial parent; and details on case status and demographics.

- Data from the Department of Protective and Regulatory Services, including substantiated instances of child abuse and/or neglect, and foster care placements made for children of study participants.

Statewide Survey of TANF Leavers

A statewide, randomly selected sample of 1,596 families leaving TANF in July through September 2000 and remaining off TANF for at least two months was surveyed approximately six months after the families left TANF. Of this group, 45 percent of the original sample (723) and 70 percent of those actually receiving the survey responded to it. Researchers determined that 581 of the original 1,596 families had moved, and verified from administrative data that respondents closely resembled the universe from which they were drawn.

Qualitative Analysis and Intensive Interviews

Research staff conducted intensive in-person interviews with 179 persons in six different research sites at some point during the fifteen months after TANF exit. These interviews provided examples of families' experiences that more fully explained the results from the statewide statistical analyses conducted on other data sources.

Econometric Analysis

To determine the factors associated with leaving TANF, being employed, and returning to TANF, several regression analyses were developed for two cohorts of TANF leavers to measure factors associated with the probability of TANF exit, the probability of employment, and the probability of returning to TANF. (Appendix B includes tables of the regressions from which this report draws.) Predictor variables included a number of demographic, program-specific, employment, and county-level economic variables.

Demographics of Research Populations

From April 1998 through June 1999 (Cohort 1), 143,491 caretaker-headed TANF cases were closed in Texas, while 23,113 similar families left TANF from July through September 2000 (Cohort 2). Ninety-four percent of Texas families leaving TANF were headed by single females. Nearly 40 percent of these parents were less than twenty-five years old, while another third were between twenty-six and thirty-four years old. Nearly half (45 percent) were Hispanic, with the remainder about evenly divided between Black and white caretakers. Most families had two children, with the youngest child being less than five years old. Half of the caretakers in families leaving TANF had completed high school. The characteristics of TANF leavers did not vary much between the two cohorts identified for this study.

Administrative Data

The demographics of the families discussed above were calculated from administrative data collected for the operation of the TANF program in Texas.

Although most characteristics of TANF leavers did not vary much between the two time periods measured (Table A.2), two differences should be noted. First, the geographic distribution of leavers shifted between the two time periods, with families in large Metropolitan Statistical Area (MSA) (highly urbanized) counties constituting a higher share of all leavers in the Cohort 1 time period (52.4 percent) than in the later time period (49.7 percent). Also, Cohort 2 leavers had been employed a greater share of the time in the prior two years (45 percent) than had Cohort 1 leavers (38 percent).

The demographic characteristics of families leaving TANF differed somewhat from the pre–welfare reform era. In that time period, Black families, those who were not high school graduates, those lacking prior work experience, and those with more than one child were all less likely to leave TANF. Also, the average age of the youngest child among TANF leavers was seven years, compared to five years for the caseload as a whole.[1]

Statewide Survey of TANF Leavers

Overall, 723 respondents completed the mail-telephone survey. The demographics of the mail-telephone survey paralleled those of the administrative data set in gender, age, and ethnic distribution (Table A.3). The average number of years of education for the survey respondents was 10.1. Fourteen percent of the participants reported eight or fewer years of formal schooling, 38 percent between nine and eleven years of schooling, 22 percent reported twelve years of schooling, and 24 percent reported some post–high school education.

At the time of the survey, 21 percent of the survey participants were married, 30 percent were separated, divorced, or widowed, and 36 percent had never been married.

Table A.2. Demographics of TANF Leavers: Comparison of Cohort 1 and Cohort 2

	Cohort 1 (N = 143,491 families)	Cohort 2 (N = 23,113 families)
Gender of primary caretaker		
Male	6.6%	6.3%
Female	93.4%	93.7%
Age of primary caretaker		
Average age (yr)	29.9	29.6
18–25	38.1%	40.0%
26–34	34.4%	34.1%
35–44	20.0%	18.9%
≥45	7.5%	7.0%
Race of primary caretaker		
Black	29.4%	28.8%
Hispanic	45.2%	45.4%
White	24.5%	24.9%
Other	0.9%	0.9%
Primary caretaker's educational level		
No high school education	16.4%	15.7%
Some high school education	33.3%	35.5%
Graduated from high school (or GED)	50.3%	48.8%
Geography		
Urban—county with large MSA	52.4%	49.7%
Suburban—county with other MSA	27.4%	27.4%
Rural—county with no MSA	20.2%	22.8%
Primary caretaker's work history		
Percent time employed in prior 2 years	38.1%	44.5%
Type of family		
Single-parent families	91.1%	90.7%
Two-parent families	8.9%	9.3%
Number of children		
Average number of children	2.0	2.0
Families with one child	41.0%	43.6%
Families with two children	31.3%	30.3%
Families with three or more children	27.6%	26.1%
Ages of children		
Average age of youngest child (yr)	4.7	4.5
Average age of all children (yr)	6.2	6.0

Source: Administrative data on those leaving TANF in the period April 1998–June 1999 (Cohort 1) or in the period July–September 2000 (Cohort 2).

Table A.3. Demographics of Statewide Survey Respondents

Number of respondents: 723

Variable observed	Percent
Gender	
Female	93.6%
Male	5.9%
Age of respondents (yr)	
18–25	36.0%
26–35	36.9%
36+	27.0%
Average age (yr)	30.3
Race/ethnicity of respondents	
Hispanic or Latino	45.1%
African-American/black	27.5%
White/Caucasian	26.8%
Asian or Pacific Islander	1.7%
Other	2.2%
Marital status of respondents	
Never been married	35.7%
Married and living with spouse	21.3%
Separated from spouse	16.6%
Divorced	11.9%
Married and living apart from spouse (in the military, on a job, or in prison)	4.6%
Widowed	1.5%
Other	7.6%
Respondent's educational level	
≤8 years	14.0%
9–11 years	37.6%
12 years	31.3%
Some post-high school	24.2%

Source: Statewide TANF leavers survey July–September 2000.

The number of children per respondent ranged from zero to ten (average, 2.2). The average age of the youngest child of the respondent was 7.8 years, but the ages ranged from one to forty-two years.[2] As expected with a more stable population, the survey recipients were somewhat older and more likely to be married than the population as a whole (see Table A.3).

Comparison of Statewide Survey and Interviews to Entire Population

Statistical comparisons were conducted to determine the similarities between the TANF leavers who responded to the statewide survey and the universe of Cohort 2 TANF leavers from administrative data. Surveyed TANF leavers bore a striking resemblance to the statewide populations from which they were randomly selected. Minor differences between the sample and the statewide population included smaller shares of leavers aged eighteen to twenty-five years and single-parent families among survey respondents than were present in the entire population. Surveyed leavers also received government benefits more often in the year prior to exit, which may have made them a bit easier to locate.

Among interviewed TANF leavers from the earlier time period, two-parent families were slightly overrepresented; otherwise their demographics were quite similar to those calculated from administrative data files. Observed differences in outcomes also appear consistent with the finding that the persons interviewed were less mobile than the population from which they were drawn.[3]

Regression Tables

This appendix presents the larger regression tables from which the report draws, particularly in Chapter 6, which explores the meaning and significance of the regressions used for the econometric analysis.

The basic approach used with each regression, with some exceptions discussed in the technical report (Schexnayder, Lein, et al., 2002), began with assembling a set of predictor variables believed to have theoretical or policy relevance for the outcome of interest. Additional variables (such as demographics and local environment) were then included so that their effects would be held constant and they could not be said to account for the relationships between the remaining predictors and the dependent variable. Because of the very large number of potential regressors available, a stepwise procedure was then utilized to reduce the list of predictors to only those with the strongest associations, accounting for significant unique variance in the dependent variable.

Both ordinary least squares (OLS) and the arguably more appropriate logistic regressions were conducted. However, owing to the computational intensity of the logistic regression estimation procedure, the stepwise procedure (which can involve many iterations) was done only with the OLS regressions. Once the final set of variables to be included had been selected by the stepwise OLS regressions, logistic regressions were conducted using the same set of predictors. The outcome of these logistic regressions was used only to confirm that the results of the OLS estimation were stable and not misleading estimates due solely to possible violation of some of the distributional assumptions inherent in the OLS regression models. The results are shown in Tables B.1 through B.4 (these tables are also available in the technical report from this project [Schexnayder, Lein, et al., 2002]).

Table B.1. Statewide TANF Recipients: Stepwise Regressions Predicting Exit from TANF

Cohort 1 (April 1998–June 1999): Dependent mean = .16; N = 971,176; R² = .04
Cohort 2 (July–September 2000): Dependent mean = .16; N = 132,720; R² = .04

Category	Variable description	Cohort 1 parameter estimate	Cohort 2 parameter estimate
	Model intercept	.173	.237
Demographics	Caretaker race is Black	−.022	−.028
	Caretaker race is Hispanic	−.020	−.024
	Caretaker race is Asian, Pacific Islander, American Indian, Alaskan Native, or unknown	−.018	
	Caretaker gender is male	.005	
	Two-parent family (TANF-UP)	.052	.057
	Caretaker education and work history indicate readiness for employment (tier 1)	−.007	
	Caretaker education and work history indicate serious impediments to employment (tier 3)		.016
	Average age of children in case	.001	
TANF experience	Percent of time receiving TANF in prior 12 months	.016	−.032
	Any non-workforce penalty received in last 3 months	.016	.024
	Current workforce-related penalty	.019	
	Any workforce-related penalty received in last 3 months	.019	.023
	Caretaker near TANF time limit (within 3 months)	.017	
	Caretaker somewhat near TANF time limit (4–6 months)		−.019
Employment services	Choices participation beyond assessment during current TANF spell	.006	.025

Table B.1. *Continued*

Cohort 1 (April 1998–June 1999): Dependent mean = .16; N = 971,176; R^2 = .04
Cohort 2 (July–September 2000): Dependent mean = .16; N = 132,720; R^2 = .04

Category	Variable description	Cohort 1 parameter estimate	Cohort 2 parameter estimate
	Choices participation, but only assessment, during current TANF spell	−.017	−.017
	Non-Choices employment services received during current TANF spell	−.047	.016
	Caretaker exempt from registration for employment services, due to caring for child	.012	.034
	Caretaker exempt from registration for employment services, due to other reasons		.032
	Caretaker refused to register for employment services	.044	.058
Employment	Currently employed (any earnings; monthly figure estimated from quarterly earnings)	.099	.067
	Current monthly earnings (monthly figure estimated from quarterly earnings)	.009	.007
	Percent of time employed (any earnings) in prior 24 months	.022	.025
	Average monthly earnings over prior 24 months	−.003	−.003
Other benefits	Percent of time any children receiving Medicaid in prior 12 months	−.021	−.120
	Percent of time receiving food stamps in prior 12 months	−.018	−.037
	Any subsidized child care received during current TANF spell	.021	

Table B.1. *Continued*

Cohort 1 (April 1998–June 1999): Dependent mean = .16; N = 971,176; R² = .04
Cohort 2 (July–September 2000): Dependent mean = .16; N = 132,720; R² = .04

Category	Variable description	Cohort 1 parameter estimate	Cohort 2 parameter estimate
Other programs	Percent of time child support payments received in prior 12 months	−.016	
	Monthly average child support receipt for prior 12 months	.021	.010
	Substantiated investigations of abuse or neglect for any children in prior 3 months	.048	.053
	Foster care placement made for any children in prior 3 months	.306	.464
County-level economic variables	High-population-density county (large MSA)	−.007	
	Population growth rate from 1990 to 2000 (%)	.00022	
	Employment growth rate from 2000 to 2001 (%)	−.003	−.003
	Unemployment rate in 2000 (%)	−.002	−.001

Source: UTRMC regressions using administrative data for all TANF recipients in the periods April 1998–June 1999 and July–September 2000

Table B.2. Statewide TANF Leavers: Stepwise Regressions Predicting UI Employment Using Administrative Data (Model 1)

Cohort 1 (April 1998–June 1999): Dependent mean = .56; N = 1,777,878; R^2 = .20
Cohort 2 (July–September 2000): Dependent mean = .56; N = 132,211; R^2 = .23

Category	Variable description	Cohort 1 parameter estimate	Cohort 2 parameter estimate
	Model intercept	.318	.369
Demographics	Caretaker age in years	−.003	−.007
	Caretaker age squared		.00005
	Caretaker race is Black	.064	.028
	Caretaker race is Hispanic	.047	.041
	Caretaker race is Asian, Pacific Islander, American Indian, Alaskan Native, or unknown	−.017	
	Caretaker gender is male	−.004	−.016
	Two-parent family (TANF-UP)	−.072	−.048
	Caretaker education of eighth grade or less	−.020	−.033
	Caretaker has graduated from high school	.013	.021
	Caretaker education and work history indicate readiness for employment (tier 1)	−.034	
	Caretaker education and work history indicate serious impediments to employment (tier 3)	.017	
	Age of youngest child in case	−.002	
	Average age of children in case	.001	
	Number of children in case	−.004	
TANF experience	Number of months since last TANF receipt (log transformed)	.024	−.022
	As of last month on TANF, percent of time receiving TANF in prior 12 months		.075
	As of last month on TANF, any non-workforce penalty received in prior 3 months	−.020	−.010

Table B.2. *Continued*

Cohort 1 (April 1998–June 1999): Dependent mean = .56; N = 1,777,878; R² = .20
Cohort 2 (July–September 2000): Dependent mean = .56; N = 132,211; R² = .23

Category	Variable description	Cohort 1 parameter estimate	Cohort 2 parameter estimate
	As of last month on TANF, any workforce-related penalty received in prior 3 months	−.027	
	Caretaker somewhat near TANF time limit (4–6 months)	−.006	
Employment services	Choices participation beyond assessment during prior TANF spell	.092	.123
	Choices participation, but only assessment, during prior TANF spell	−.006	−.022
	Non-Choices employment services received during prior TANF spell	.027	
	Caretaker exempt from registration for employment services, due to caring for child	−.028	.021
	Caretaker exempt from registration for employment services, due to other reasons	−.075	
	Caretaker refused to register for employment services	−.014	−.016
Employment	Percent of time employed (any earnings) in prior 24 months	.572	.579
	Average monthly earnings over prior 24 months	.004	.002
Other benefits	Any Medicaid receipt during off-TANF spell	.040	.030
	Medicaid receipt for any children during off-TANF spell	.088	.065
	Any food stamps receipt during off-TANF spell	.004	−.015
	Any subsidized child care receipt during off-TANF spell	.130	.085

Table B.2. *Continued*

Cohort 1 (April 1998–June 1999): Dependent mean = .56; N = 1,777,878; R² = .20
Cohort 2 (July–September 2000): Dependent mean = .56; N = 132,211; R² = .23

Category	Variable description	Cohort 1 parameter estimate	Cohort 2 parameter estimate
	As of last month on TANF, percent of time receiving Medicaid in prior 12 months	.047	
	As of last month on TANF, percent of time any children receiving Medicaid in prior 12 months	.037	
	As of last month on TANF, percent of time receiving food stamps in prior 12 months	.009	
	Any subsidized child care received during prior TANF spell		.045
Other programs	Percent of time child support payments received in prior 12 months	.009	
	Monthly average child support receipt for prior 12 months	−.011	−.011
	Substantiated investigations of abuse or neglect for any children in prior 3 months	−.037	
County-level economic variables	High-population-density county (large MSA)	.015	
	Low-population-density county (no MSA)	.022	.018
	Employment growth rate from 2000 to 2001 (%)		−.002
	Unemployment rate in 2000 (%)	−.006	−.005

Source: UTRMC regression analysis using administrative data for all TANF recipients in the periods April 1998–June 1999 and July–September 2000

Table B.3. Surveyed TANF Leavers: Stepwise Regressions Predicting UI Employment Using Both Administrative and Survey Data (Model 2)

Statewide sample, administrative data: Dependent mean = .55; N = 39,019; R^2 = .27
Survey sample, administrative data: Dependent mean = .57; N = 682; R^2 = .34
Administrative plus survey data: Dependent mean = .57; N = 678; R^2 = .43

Category	Variable description	Statewide sample: Administrative data only, parameter estimate	Survey sample: Administrative data only, parameter estimate	Administrative data plus survey, parameter estimate
	Model intercept	.306	.254	.321
Demographics	Caretaker age (yr)	−.006		
	Caretaker age (yr) squared	.00004		
	Caretaker race is Black	.023		
	Caretaker race is Hispanic	.032		
	Two-parent family (TANF-UP)	−.062	−.111	
	Caretaker education of eighth grade or less	−.025		
	Caretaker has graduated from high school	.018		
TANF experience	As of last month on TANF, percent of time receiving TANF in prior 12 months	.050		
Employment services	Choices participation beyond assessment during prior TANF spell	.111	.120	
	Non-Choices employment services received during prior TANF spell		.140	.105

Table B.3. *Continued*

Statewide sample, administrative data: Dependent mean = .55; N = 39,019; R² = .27
Survey sample, administrative data: Dependent mean = .57; N = 682; R² = .34
Administrative plus survey data: Dependent mean = .57; N = 678; R² = .43

Category	Variable description	Statewide sample: Administrative data only, parameter estimate	Survey sample: Administrative data only, parameter estimate	Administrative data plus survey, parameter estimate
	Caretaker exempt from registration for employment services, due to caring for child	.029		
Employment	As of last month on TANF, percent of time employed (any earnings) in prior 24 months	.541	.596	.515
	As of last month on TANF, average monthly earnings over prior 24 months	.002		
Other benefits	Any Medicaid receipt during off-TANF spell	.021		
	Medicaid receipt for any children during off-TANF spell	.097	.131	.129
	Any subsidized child care receipt during off-TANF spell	.136	.229	.240
	As of last month on TANF, percent of time any children receiving Medicaid in prior 12 months		−.306	

Table B.3. *Continued*

Statewide sample, administrative data: Dependent mean = .55; N = 39,019; R² = .27
Survey sample, administrative data: Dependent mean = .57; N = 682; R² = .34
Administrative plus survey data: Dependent mean = .57; N = 678; R² = .43

Category	Variable description	Statewide sample: Administrative data only, parameter estimate	Survey sample: Administrative data only, parameter estimate	Administrative data plus survey, parameter estimate
Other programs	Percent of time child support payments received in 6 months following TANF exit	−.029		
County-level economic variables	Low population-density county (no MSA)	.016		
	Unemployment rate 2000 (%)	−.004		−.008
Survey: demographics	Married and living with spouse			−.124
	Widowed			−.270
Survey: income	Looked for work in the past 6 months			.090
	Income assistance from TANF in the past six months			−.082
Survey: TANF	Exited TANF because of child support receipt			−.133
	Exited TANF because could not provide necessary documentation			−.227
	Returned to TANF because of divorce or separation			−.171

Table B.3. *Continued*

Statewide sample, administrative data: Dependent mean = .55; N = 39,019; R² = .27
Survey sample, administrative data: Dependent mean = .57; N = 682; R² = .34
Administrative plus survey data: Dependent mean = .57; N = 678; R² = .43

Category	Variable description	Statewide sample: Administrative data only, parameter estimate	Survey sample: Administrative data only, parameter estimate	Administrative data plus survey, parameter estimate
Survey: health	Children needed to see a doctor but couldn't afford to			.100
Survey: transportation	Reliability of usual transportation			.090
Survey: child care	Care for youngest child myself			−.123
	Youngest child cared for by babysitter or other nonrelative at that person's home			.117
Survey: dealing with problems	Family or friends have helped with transportation in past 6 months			−.089
	Over past 6 months, have lived with family or friends			−.073
Survey: multiple areas	Experienced barriers to employment in two or more areas (child care, health, transportation)			−.092

Source: UTRMC regression analysis using administrative and survey data for families leaving TANF in July–September 2000.

Table B.4. Survey of TANF Leavers: Stepwise Regressions Predicting Reentry to TANF Using Administrative and Survey Data Combined (Model 2)

Statewide sample, administrative data: Dependent mean = .30; N = 38,746; R² = .11
Survey sample, administrative data: Dependent mean = .24; N = 681; R² = .13
Administrative plus survey data: Dependent mean = .24; N = 677; R² = .32

Category	Variable description	*Statewide sample: Administrative data only, parameter estimate*	*Survey sample: Administrative data only, parameter estimate*	*Survey sample: Administrative data only, parameter estimate*
	Model intercept	.468	.251	.390
Demographics	Caretaker age (yr)	−.007		
	Caretaker age (yr) squared	.00007		
	Caretaker race is Black	.086	.094	
	Caretaker race is Hispanic	.016		
	Two-parent family (TANF-UP)	−.063		
	Caretaker education and work history indicate readiness for employment (tier 1)	.026		
	Caretaker education and work history indicate serious impediments to employment (tier 3)	−.042	−.096	−.087
	Age of youngest child on case	−.005		
	Number of children on case	.013		.028
TANF experience	As of last month on TANF, percent of time receiving TANF in prior 12 months	.040		

Table B.4. *Continued*

Statewide sample, administrative data: Dependent mean = .30; N = 38,746; R^2 = .11
Survey sample, administrative data: Dependent mean = .24; N = 681; R^2 = .13
Administrative plus survey data: Dependent mean = .24; N = 677; R^2 = .32

Category	Variable description	Statewide sample: Administrative data only, parameter estimate	Survey sample: Administrative data only, parameter estimate	Survey sample: Administrative data only, parameter estimate
	As of last month on TANF, any work-force-related penalty received in prior 3 months	.026		
	Caretaker near TANF time limit (within 3 months)	−.040		
Employment services	Choices participation beyond assessment during prior TANF spell	−.037		
	Caretaker exempt from registration for em-ployment services, due to caring for child	−.126		
	Caretaker exempt from registration for em-ployment services, due to other reasons	−.091		−.104
	Caretaker refused to register for employ-ment services	−.080	−.087	−.131
Employment	Earnings in exit month (monthly figure esti-mated from quarterly earnings)	−.012	−.020	−.014

Table B.4. *Continued*

Statewide sample, administrative data: Dependent mean = .30; N = 38,746; R^2 = .11
Survey sample, administrative data: Dependent mean = .24; N = 681; R^2 = .13
Administrative plus survey data: Dependent mean = .24; N = 677; R^2 = .32

Category	Variable description	Statewide sample: Administrative data only, parameter estimate	Survey sample: Administrative data only, parameter estimate	Survey sample: Administrative data only, parameter estimate
	As of last month on TANF, percent of time employed (any earnings) in prior 24 months	.040	.227	.225
	As of last month on TANF, average monthly earnings over prior 24 months	.005		
Other benefits	Any Medicaid receipt during off-TANF spell	.190		
	Medicaid receipt for any children during off-TANF spell	−.191		
	Any food stamps receipt during off-TANF spell	−.018	−.131	−.109
	Any subsidized child care receipt during off-TANF spell	−.027		
	As of last month on TANF, percent of time receiving Medicaid in prior 12 months	.044		

Table B.4. *Continued*

Statewide sample, administrative data: Dependent mean = .30; N = 38,746; R^2 = .11
Survey sample, administrative data: Dependent mean = .24; N = 681; R^2 = .13
Administrative plus survey data: Dependent mean = .24; N = 677; R^2 = .32

Category	Variable description	*Statewide sample: Administrative data only, parameter estimate*	*Survey sample: Administrative data only, parameter estimate*	*Survey sample: Administrative data only, parameter estimate*
	As of last month on TANF, percent of time receiving food stamps in prior 12 months	.104	.167	.118
	Any subsidized child care received during prior TANF spell	.036	.078	.083
Other programs	Percent of time child support payments received in 6 months following TANF exit	−.056		
	Monthly average child support receipt for 6 months following TANF exit	−.040	−.069	−.060
	Substantiated investigations of abuse or neglect for any children	.682		
County-level economic variables	Low-population-density county (no MSA)	.037		
Survey: demographics	Widowed			−.248

Table B.4. *Continued*

Statewide sample, administrative data: Dependent mean = .30; N = 38,746; R² = .11
Survey sample, administrative data: Dependent mean = .24; N = 681; R² = .13
Administrative plus survey data: Dependent mean = .24; N = 677; R² = .32

Category	Variable description	Statewide sample: Administrative data only, parameter estimate	Survey sample: Administrative data only, parameter estimate	Survey sample: Administrative data only, parameter estimate
Survey: employment	Currently employed			−.252
Survey: income	Any income from Unemployment Insurance last month			−.198
Survey: TANF	Exited TANF because got married			−.233
	Exited TANF because another adult contributed money			−.152
	Exited TANF because obtained reliable transportation			−.160
Survey: health	Needed to see a doctor but couldn't afford to			−.134
Survey: transportation	Own or share a car or truck			−.095
Survey: food	Received food assistance from school lunch program in past 6 months			.074

Table B.4. *Continued*

Statewide sample, administrative data: Dependent mean = .30; N = 38,746; R² = .11
Survey sample, administrative data: Dependent mean = .24; N = 681; R² = .13
Administrative plus survey data: Dependent mean = .24; N = 677; R² = .32

Category	Variable description	*Statewide sample: Administrative data only, parameter estimate*	*Survey sample: Administrative data only, parameter estimate*	*Survey sample: Administrative data only, parameter estimate*
Survey: housing	Received any assistance with housing costs in past 6 months			.113
	Received assistance with fuel costs in past 6 months			.339
	Received assistance with telephone costs in past 6 months			−.183
Survey: child care	Youngest child cared for by babysitter or other nonrelative at that person's home			.138
Survey: dealing with problems	Over past 6 months, have been unable to afford rent			.081

Source: RMC regression analysis using administrative and survey data for families leaving TANF in the period July–September 2000.

Chapter 1

1 PRWORA only exempted parents with children less than one year old. These restrictions were designed to prepare the state of Texas for the expiration of its waiver in 2002.

2 Before September 2003, Texas sanctioned only the adult caretakers in a TANF household for failure to comply with personal responsibility agreement (PRA) requirements. When an adult failed to comply with work or child-support cooperation requirements, the adult's portion of the family's cash assistance was terminated. For noncompliance with any of the other program requirements, the client was sanctioned a fixed dollar amount for each infraction. For example, a parent was sanctioned $25 a month for each child not meeting school attendance requirements. Under the full-family sanction policy adopted in September 2003, the family lost all of its TANF assistance when a parent violated any requirement of the PRA. The Health and Human Services Commission estimates that 17,511 fewer families received TANF each month in fiscal 2004 as a result of the full-family sanction policy. Only one-third of sanctioned families, on average, return to the TANF program within six months of the sanction (Hagert, 2005).

Chapter 2

1 Although the state of Texas devolved some policies, particularly those related to subsidized child care, to the local level, local variations in TANF policy had little effect on welfare leavers at the time of our study, 1999–2001 (Schexnayder, Lein, et al., 2002).

2 Unless otherwise indicated, all quantitative data in this section come from the U.S. Census and the U.S. Department of Labor 2003 report, *Employment Characteristics of Families in 2002.* Census sources include "State and County Quick Facts" (2000), "Low Income Uninsured Children by State" (1998–2000), and "Educational Attainment" (2003). More qualitative assessments of life in these areas came from observations by members of the research team in the course of the research and reports by our respondents during the interviews.

3 The information in this section comes from Murdock et al. (2002).

4 This profile of the Texas economy draws from information provided by the Texas Workforce Commission (2001, 2002).

Chapter 3

1 The study took place prior to the implementation of the Children's Health Insurance Program (CHIP) in Texas.

2 Although other rules also apply to the FSE&T program, the ones reported above are those most likely to apply to the study population.

3 As the majority of the research sites were FSE&T active sites, with services available, respondents who were not exempt from FSE&T program requirements or who were already participating in the Choices program would indeed have to be employed or engaged in other eligible activities.

4 There are certainly likely to be eligible households who do not wish to get benefits even if

they are eligible. Such households would not appear in our sample unless they were willing to accept TANF benefits at some time.

Chapter 4

1 This research took place before the Children's Health Insurance Program (CHIP) was implemented in Texas.

2 Our study does not provide evidence of the importance of the Earned Income Tax Credit. Only 3.3 percent of the survey respondents reported receiving it. However, respondents were asked about income for the previous six months, and the survey was fielded more than six months after the most recent income tax deadline.

3 Prior to April 2000, any child support arrears collected after families left TANF were used to reimburse the state for past TANF payments first, before being distributed to custodial parents.

4 Child support payments for middle-income families are usually handled by local or private agencies rather than the Office of the Attorney General.

5 Unlike other measures, child support could only be tracked six months prior to diversion or exit, owing to the implementation of a new child support data system in the fall of 1997.

6 Will Rogers, Texas Office of the Attorney General, personal communication, October 2001.

7 See Urban Institute (2001b). The NSAF included those who had ever received AFDC/TANF in its definition of former TANF recipients, whereas our report focuses on recent TANF leavers.

Chapter 5

1 These findings were not duplicated in the regression findings, which also examined factors associated with return to TANF.

Chapter 6

1 Although we tracked Cohort 2 leavers for only six months, the rates of return to TANF were actually higher for these families than for Cohort 1 families.

2 Schexnayder et al. (1998) measured an exit rate of 12 percent per month for AFDC caretakers. Differences in definition of leavers (caretakers instead of cases) may have accounted for some of the differences.

3 This is a coded category from administrative databases. As discussed earlier, the qualitative interviews revealed complex reasons why caretakers might not have been registered with employment services.

4 To a lesser degree, families in which the mother was employed more often over the past two years, families that were exempt from Choices participation because of having a very young child, or families that had received larger than average child support payments in the preceding twelve months also left TANF at a higher rate.

5 These variables, while statistically associated with employment, may or may not actually cause persons to become employed.

6 A number of additional regressions not discussed here were used to make sure that dif-

ferences between the two models were not caused by the differences in time periods or sample size. The major findings discussed in this chapter held true in all of the variations of the models discussed.

7 This finding should be interpreted cautiously because for some, employment was a necessary condition for receipt of subsidized child care.

8 These two predictors are highly correlated ($r = 0.56$, N = 678) in the combined sample.

9 In Appendix Table B.4, in the columns labeled "Statewide: Administrative data only," having Medicaid for children was also associated with staying off TANF, but not strongly enough to be significant with the smaller sample in other regression models. It is possible that the variable "Needing Medicaid for self or children" (Table 6.5) measures the same thing but is a more precise variable than mere enrollment in Medicaid.

Appendix A

1 See Schexnayder et al. (1998) for a discussion of Texas welfare dynamics prior to reform. Strict comparisons cannot be made because earlier studies measured caretaker exits, whereas this study measured exits by the entire case.

2 The age of the youngest child is higher than calculated from administrative data both because of the presence of respondents whose own children were adults and because of differences in the definition of this measure between the two data sources. The administrative data included only those children on the TANF grant, whereas our survey included all children of the respondent.

3 See the technical report by Schexnayder, Lein, and colleagues (2002) for a discussion of the effect of mobility on the interview sample and for a more complete discussion of the characteristics of the interview sample.

Acs, Gregory, and Pamela Loprest. 2001. *Initial Synthesis Report of the Findings from ASPE's "Leavers" Grants.* Washington, DC: Urban Institute.

Angel, Ronald, Laura Lein, and Jane Henrici. 2006. *Poor Families in America's Health Care Crisis.* New York: Cambridge University Press.

Angel, Ronald, Laura Lein, Jane Henrici, and Emily Leventhal. 2001. *Health Insurance Coverage for Children and Their Caregivers in Low-Income Urban Neighborhoods.* Policy Brief 01-2, Report of Welfare, Children, and Families: A Three-City Study. Baltimore: Johns Hopkins University.

Baj, John, Julie L. Hotchkiss, Christopher T. King, Peter R. Mueser, Phillip S. Rokicki, and David W. Stevens. 2001. *Urban Welfare-to-Work Transition in the 1990s: Patterns in Six Urban Areas.* Washington, DC: U.S. Department of Labor, Employment and Training Administration, Office of Policy and Research, Division of Research and Demonstration.

Bane, Mary Jo, and David T. Ellwood. 1986. "Slipping Into and Out of Poverty: The Dynamics of Spells." *Journal of Human Resources* 21(1): 1–23.

Bean, Frank, Jennifer V. W. Van Hook, and Jennifer E. Glick. 1997. "Country of Origin, Type of Public Assistance, and Patterns of Welfare Recipiency among U.S. Immigrants and Natives." *Social Science Quarterly* 78:432–451.

Bloom, Dan, Richard Hendra, Karin Martinson, and Susan Scrivener. 2005. *The Employment Retention and Advancement Project: Early Results from Four Sites.* New York: MDRC.

Borjas, George J. 2000. "The Economic Progress of Immigrants." In *Issues in the Economics of Immigration,* ed. George J. Borjas, 15–49. Chicago: University of Chicago Press.

Boushey, Heather, and David Rosnick. 2003. "Jobs Held by Former Welfare Recipients Hit Hard by Economic Downturn." Washington, DC: Center for Economic and Policy Research. http://www.cepr.net/publications/TANF.htm (last accessed January 29, 2005).

Burton, Linda M., and Keith A. Whitfield. 2003. "Weathering Towards Poorer Health in Later Life: Co-Morbidity in Urban Low-Income Families." *Public Policy and Aging Report* 13, no. 3. Washington, DC: National Academy on an Aging Society.

Camarota, Steven A. 2001. *The Slowing Progress of Immigrants: An Examination of Income, Home Ownership, and Citizenship, 1970-2000.* Washington, DC: Center for Immigration Studies.

Cappelli, Peter, Laurie Bassi, Harry Katz, David Knoke, Paul Osterman, and Michael
    Useem. 1997. *Change at Work*. New York: Oxford University Press.
Cauthen, Nancy K. 2002. *Improving Children's Economic Security: Research Findings
    About Increasing Family Income Through Employment*. Policy Brief no. 2, *Earned
    Income Tax Credits*. New York: Columbia University, National Center for Children
    in Poverty.
Cawley, John, and Sheldon H. Danziger. 2005. "Does It Pay to Move from Welfare to
    Work? Reply to Robert Moffitt and Katie Winder." *Journal of Policy Analysis and
    Management* 24(2): 411–417.
Center for Public Policy Priorities. 1999. "Most Poor Texas Families Work." http://
    www.cppp.org/products/media/pressreleases/PRwbp.html (last accessed March
    25, 2005).
———. 2003. Family Security Index. http://www.cppp.org/products/fsi.html (last
    accessed March 25, 2005).
Chase-Lansdale, P. Lindsay, Rebekah Levine Coley, Brenda J. Lohman, and Laura D.
    Pittman. 2002. *Welfare Reform: What About the Children?* Policy Brief 02-1, Report
    of Welfare, Children, and Families: A Three-City Study. Baltimore: Johns Hopkins
    University.
Collins, Ann, Fred Glantz, J. Lee Kreader, Jean Layzer, and Alan Werner. 2000.
    *National Study of Child Care for Low-Income Families: State and Community
    Substudy Interim Report*. New York: Abt Associates and National Center for
    Children in Poverty.
Danziger, Sheldon, Colleen M. Heflin, Mary E. Corcoran, Elizabeth Oltmans, and
    Hui-Chen Wang. 2002. "Does It Pay to Move from Welfare to Work?" *Journal of
    the Association for Policy Analysis and Management* 21:671–692.
Earle, Alison, and S. Jody Heymann. 2002. "What Causes Job Loss among Former
    Welfare Recipients: The Role of Family Health Problems." *Journal of the American
    Medical Women's Association* 57:5–10.
Edin, Kathryn, and Laura Lein. 1997. *Making Ends Meet*. New York: Russell Sage
    Foundation.
Fix, Michael, and Jeffrey S. Passel. 1994. *Immigration and Immigrants: Setting the
    Record Straight*. Washington, DC: Urban Institute.
———. 1999. *Trends in Noncitizens' and Citizens' Use of Public Benefits Following
    Welfare Reform, 1994–1997*. Washington, DC: Urban Institute.
Hagert, Celia. 2005. "What's Happening with TANF Caseloads: Strict Rules Force
    Thousands of Kids off the Rolls." Austin, TX: Center for Public Policy Priorities.
    http://www.cppp.org/research.php?aid=104&cid=3&scid=12 (last accessed March
    15, 2005).

Henly, Julia R., and Sandra Lyons. 2000. "The Negotiations of Child Care and
Employment Demands among Low-Income Parents." *Journal of Social Issues*
56(4): 683–705.

Heymann, S. Jody, and Alison Earle. 1999. "The Impact of Welfare Reform on Parents'
Ability to Care for Their Children's Health." *American Journal of Public Health*
89(4): 502–526.

International Labour Office. 1998. *World Employment Report, 1989–1999:
Employability in the Global Economy: How Training Matters.* Geneva: ILO.

Instituto Nacional de Estadística, Geografía e Informática, Mexico. http://www.inegi.
gob.mx/inegi/default.asp (last accessed March 26, 2005).

Isaacs, Julie, and Matthew Lyon. 2000. "A Cross-State Examination of Families
Leaving Welfare: Findings from the ASPE-Funded Leavers Studies." Washington,
DC: U.S. Department of Health and Human Services, Office of the Assistant
Secretary for Planning and Evaluation. http://aspe.hhs.gov/hsp/leavers99/cross-
state00/index.htm (last accessed February 22, 2006).

Judy, Richard W., and Carol D'Amico. 1997. *Workforce 2020: Work and Workers in the
21st Century.* Indianapolis: Hudson Institute.

King, Christopher T., and Peter R. Mueser. 2005. *Welfare and Work: Experiences in Six
Cities.* Kalamazoo, MI: W. E. Upjohn Institute for Employment Research.

King, Christopher T., and Daniel Schroeder. 2003. *The Role of Child Support and
Earnings in Texas Welfare and Poverty Dynamics.* Ray Marshall Center for the
Study of Human Resources, University of Texas at Austin.

King, Christopher T., Deanna T. Schexnayder, and Jerome A. Olson. 1991. *A Baseline
Analysis of the Factors Influencing AFDC Duration and Labor Market Outcomes.*
Ray Marshall Center for the Study of Human Resources and Bureau of Business
Research, University of Texas at Austin.

Lambert, Susan, Elaine Waxman, and Anna Haley-Lock. 2002. "Against the Odds: A
Study of Instability in Lower-skilled Jobs." University of Chicago Working Paper,
Project on the Public Economy of Work. School of Social Service Administration,
University of Chicago.

Lane, Julia, Kelly S. Mikelson, Patrick T. Sharkey, and Douglas A. Wissoker. 2001. *Low-
income and Low-Skilled Workers' Involvement in Nonstandard Employment: Final
Report.* Washington, DC: U.S. Department of Health and Human Services, Office
of the Assistant Secretary for Planning and Evaluation.

Lee, Geum-Yong, and Ronald J. Angel. 2002. "Living Arrangements and Supplemental
Security Income Use among Elderly Asians and Hispanics in the United States:
The Role of Nativity and Citizenship." *Journal of Ethnic and Migration Studies*
28(3): 553–563.

Looney, Sarah, and Deanna Schexnayder. 2004. *Impacts of Workforce Services for Young, Low-Income Fathers: Findings from the Texas Bootstrap Project.* Ray Marshall Center for the Study of Human Resources, University of Texas at Austin.

Loprest, Pamela J. 2002. "Who Returns to Welfare?" Urban Institute Series B, no. B-49. Washington, DC: Urban Institute.

———. 2003. "Use of Government Benefits Increases among Families Leaving Welfare." Washington, DC: Urban Institute. http://www.urban.org/url. efm?10=310838 (last accessed March 14, 2005).

Mathematica Policy Research, Inc. 2002. *Reaching Those in Need: Food Stamp Participation Rates in the States in 2001.* Princeton, NJ: Mathematica Policy Research, for the USDA Food and Nutrition Service.

McMillion, Robin, Jason Ramirez, and Jeff Webster. 2005. *State of Student Aid and Higher Education.* Austin: Texas Guaranteed Student Loan Corporation.

Meyers, Marcia, Ann Collins, Elizabeth Davis, Annie Georges, J. Lee Kreader, Jerry Olson, Laura Peck, Deanna Schexnayder, Daniel Schroeder, and Roberta Weber. 2002. *The Dynamics of Child Care Subsidy Use: A Collaborative Study of Five States.* New York: National Center for Children in Poverty.

Miller, Cynthia. 2002. *Leavers, Stayers, and Cyclers: An Analysis of the Welfare Caseload.* New York: MDRC.

Moffit, Robert, and Katie Winder. 2005. "Does It Pay to Move from Welfare to Work? A Comment on Danziger, Heflin, Corcoran, Oltmans and Wang." *Journal of Policy Analysis and Management* 24(2): 399–409.

Moffit, Robert, Andrew Cherlin, Linda Burton, Mark King, and Jennifer Roff. 2002. "The Characteristics of Families Remaining on Welfare." Working Paper no. 02-2. Report of Welfare, Children, and Families: A Three-City Study. Baltimore: Johns Hopkins University. http://www.jhu.edu/~welfare (last accessed September 15, 2006).

Murdock, Steve H., Steve White, Md. Naxrul Hoque, Beverly Pecotte, Xiuhong You, and Jennifer Balkan. 2002. "A Summary of the Texas Challenge in the Twenty-First Century: Implications of Population Change for the Future of Texas." Department of Rural Sociology, Texas A&M University.

National Governors Association. 2000. *State Strategies for the New Economy.* Washington, DC: National Governors Association Center for Best Practices.

Perez, Sonia M., ed. 2000. *Moving Up the Economic Ladder: Latino Workers and the Nation's Future Prosperity.* Washington, DC: National Council of La Raza.

Repetti, Rena L., Karen A. Matthews, and Ingrid Waldron. 1989. "Employment and Women's Health: Effects of Paid Employment on Women's Mental and Physical Health." *American Psychologist* 44(11): 1394–1401.

Santos, Richard, and Patricia Seitz. 2000. "Benefit Coverage for Latino and Latina

Workers." In *Moving Up the Economic Ladder: Latino Workers and the Nation's Future Prosperity,* ed. Sonia M. Perez, 162–185. Washington, DC: National Council of La Raza.

Schexnayder, Deanna, Brendan Hill, and Ying Tang. 2006. *Bridging the Gap: An Analysis of the Resources Needed to Meet a Basic Family Budget in Texas Communities.* Ray Marshall Center for the Study of Human Resources, University of Texas at Austin.

Schexnayder, Deanna T., Christopher T. King, and Jerome A. Olson. 1991. *A Baseline Analysis of Factors Influencing AFDC Duration and Labor Market Outcomes.* Ray Marshall Center for the Study of Human Resources and the Bureau of Business Research, University of Texas at Austin.

Schexnayder, Deanna T., Laura Lein, Karen Douglas, Daniel G. Schroeder, David Dominguez, and Freddie Richards. 2002. *Texas Families in Transition/Surviving Without TANF: An Analysis of Families Diverted From or Leaving TANF.* Ray Marshall Center for the Study of Human Resources and Center for Social Work Research, University of Texas at Austin.

Schexnayder, Deanna T., Jerome A. Olson, Daniel G. Schroeder, and Jody McCoy. 1998. *The Role of Child Support in Texas Welfare Dynamics.* Ray Marshall Center for the Study of Human Resources, University of Texas at Austin.

Schexnayder, Deanna, Daniel G. Schroeder, Katherine Faliski, and Jody McCoy. 1999. *Texas Subsidized Child Care Utilization Patterns and Outcomes.* Ray Marshall Center for the Study of Human Resources, University of Texas at Austin.

Schexnayder, Deanna T., Daniel G. Schroeder, Jerome A. Olson, and Hyunsub Kum. 2002. *Achieving Change for Texans Evaluation: Final Impact Report.* Ray Marshall Center for the Study of Human Resources, University of Texas at Austin.

Schroeder, Daniel, Sarah Looney, and Deanna Schexnayder. 2004. *Impacts of Workforce Services for Young Low-Income Fathers: Findings from the Texas Bootstrap Project.* Ray Marshall Center for the Study of Human Resources, University of Texas at Austin.

Shenkman, Elizabeth, Jana Col, Yue Du, Virginia Schaffer, and Delfino Vargas. 2002. *Quality of Care in the Children's Health Insurance Program in Texas.* Vol. 1, *Narrative Section.* Institute for Child Health Policy, University of Florida, Gainesville.

Smith, J. P., and Barry Edmonston. 1997. *The New Americans: Economic, Demographic and Fiscal Impacts of Immigration.* Washington, DC: National Academies Press.

Texas Department of Health. 2002. Information published by the Texas Department of State Health Services. http://www.dshs.state.tx.us/chs/cfs/ (last accessed September 10, 2006).

Texas Department of Human Services. 2000. *Annual Report.* http://www.dhs.state.

tx.us/publications/AnnualReport/2000/AR_TW_p10_18.pdf, p. 3 (last accessed March 20, 2005).

Texas Health and Human Services Commission. 2000. "Demographic Profile of the Texas Population Living in Poverty in 2000." www.hhsc.state.tx.us/research/dssi/TXPOOR2000.html (last accessed August 6, 2002).

———. 2006. News release, May 30, 2006. http:www.hhs.state.tx.us/news/release/050406_30day_reviews.shtml (last accessed September 20, 2006).

Texas Low Income Housing Service Information Service. n.d. Profile of HUD subsidized housing in Texas (from 1997 HUD database, "Picture of Subsidized Households"). http://www.texashousing.org/txlihis/index.html (last accessed April 4, 2005).

Texas Workforce Commission. 2001. *Texas Annual Employment and Earnings, 1999–2000.* Austin: Texas Workforce Commission Labor Market Information Department.

———. 2002. *The Texas Economy: An Age of Global Economic Opportunity.* Austin: Texas Workforce Commission Division of Career Development Resources.

Tienda, Marta, and Leif Jensen. 1986. "Immigration and Public Assistance Participation: Dispelling the Myth of Dependency." *Social Science Research* 15:372–400.

Trejo, Stephen J. 1992. "Immigrant Welfare Recipiency: Recent Trends and Future Implications." *Contemporary Political Issues* 10:44–53.

United States Census. "State and County Quick Facts." http://quickfacts.census.gov/qfd/states/00000.html (last accessed March 23, 2005).

United States Census. 1998–2000. "Low Income Uninsured Children by State: 1998, 1999, and 2000." http://www.census.gov/hhes/www/hlthins/lowinckid.html (last accessed February 6, 2006).

United States Census. "Educational Attainment." http://www.census.gov/population/www/socdemo/educ-attn.html (last accessed March 26, 2005).

United States Department of Labor, Bureau of Labor Statistics. 2003. *Employment Characteristics of Families in 2002.*

United States General Accounting Office. 1995. *Major Overhaul Needed to Create a More Efficient, Customer-Driven System.* Washington, DC: U.S. GAO.

United States House of Representatives, Ways and Means Committee. 2002. *Green Book.* Washington, DC: U.S. Government Printing Office.

———. 2006. "Human Resources Provisions in the Deficit Reduction Act." http://waysandmeans.house.gov/media/pdf/welfare/013006welfaretable.pdf (last accessed September 20, 2006).

United States Housing and Urban Development. 2000. "A Report on Worst Case

Housing Needs in 1999: New Opportunity Amid Continuing Challenges."
Washington, DC: HUD, Office of Policy Development and Research.

———. n.d. "Profile of HUD Subsidized Housing in Texas." Washington, DC: HUD.

Urban Institute. 2001a. *Who Graduates? Who Doesn't? A Statistical Portrait of Public
High School Graduation, Class of 2001.* Washington, DC: Urban Institute.

———. 2001b. *National Survey of America's Families.* Washington, DC: Urban
Institute.

Uttal, Lynet. 1997. "'Trust Your Instincts': Racial, Ethnic, and Class-Based Preferences
in Employed Mothers' Child Care Choices." *Qualitative Sociology* 20(2): 253–274.

———. 1999. "Using Kin for Child Care: Embedment in the Socioeconomic
Networks of Extended Families." *Journal of Marriage and the Family* 61(4):
845–857.

Van Hook, Jennifer. 2000. "SSI Eligibility and Participation among Elderly
Naturalized Citizens and Noncitizens." *Social Science Research* 29:51–69.

Van Hook, Jennifer L., and Frank D. Bean. 1998. "Welfare Reform and SSI Receipt
among Immigrants in the United States." In *Immigration, Citizenship, and the
Welfare State,* ed. Hermann Kurthen, Jürgen Fijalkowski, and Gert Wagner, 139–
157. Greenwich, CT: Jai Press.

Zedlewski, Sheila R. 2002. "Family Incomes: Rising, Falling, or Holding Steady?"
In *Welfare Reform: The Next Act,* ed. Alan Weil and Kenneth Finegold, 53–77.
Washington, DC: Urban Institute Press.